RENOVATE YOUR RELATIONSHIP

Testimonials for
Renovate Your Relationship

'*Renovate Your Relationship* is a timely, entertaining and practical handbook for relationship building, maintenance and improvement. A must-read for every couple.'

Sarah McKay DPhil (Oxon)
Neuroscientist, Speaker, Author, Media Commentator

'Intimate partnerships—marriages can be challenging and yet the best thing in our lives. Joanne Wilson's wonderful book provides a wealth of insights, not only from her professional experiences with couples but by making new developments in neuroscience relevant and practical to our relationships. Beautifully written, this book offers a comprehensive understanding of successful relationships. As she eloquently notes "Marriage is not an ancient and outdated tradition: it is a wonderful celebration of the love you have for your partner." This book is a must read for those wanting to cultivate depth, love, and longevity to their marriage.'

John Arden, PhD
author of *Mind-Brain-Gene*

'Joanne Wilson hands out tools for your marriage no matter what state it is in! Newlyweds, oldly-weds, people experiencing marriage difficulties, people with a healthy marriage—everyone will find something to make their marriage stronger. Jo obviously loves helping couples and families achieve their best, no matter what that is, and her compassion, wit and experience shine in this book. Highly recommended!'

Kristin Lucas
Married 15 years and mother of three

'Nothing short of brilliant! Jo expertly blends quirky humour with credible scientific knowledge and most importantly—tangible, real-life, hands-on strategies to improve every relationship no matter what stage you're at. This book is so REAL and made me laugh, cringe and indeed take a good hard look at the best and worst of what is going on in my own relationship. Highly recommend to all!'

Megan Jantke
Married 17 years, mother of four

'This is brilliant. There are so many great tips and practical steps for people to follow. This is going to be really helpful for so many couples, and maybe it will be the first step for many to stepping into a counselling room.'

A. Bueti
Married 30 years, mother of two

'The book is absolutely fantastic. I love the writing, I love the anecdotes and I love the way it is presented. This is my type of book, practical and with bullet points lists!'

Tammy
Single

'This book reminds us that no-one has a perfect relationship. Even the most thriving partnerships come with their challenges. Joanne gives useful, relatable and practical advice and exercises to help nurture healthy relationships. Regardless of the stage or state of your relationship, everyone will find something to take away from this entertaining and enlightening read!'

Annemarie
Married 21 years, mother of one

RENOVATE YOUR RELATIONSHIP

ALL THE DIY TOOLS YOU'LL EVER NEED
FOR YOUR MOST IMPORTANT PROJECT

JOANNE WILSON
THE RELATIONSHIP REJUVENATOR

The Relationship
REJUVENATOR

Relationship Rejuvenator Publishing™
www.relationshiprejuvenator.com

2 3 4 5 6 7 8 9 10
First edition 2020

ISBN: 978-0-646-81919-8

DEDICATION

With gratitude to the loving legacy of my parents and parents-in-law.

To my husband for a 'full marriage experience' and who made my love story come true.

I thank God for his sense of humour by answering my prayer for a beautiful man then gifting me with four.

TABLE OF CONTENTS

Table of Contents

Renovate Your Relationship

ACKNOWLEDGEMENTS

In recognition of the thought leaders in this field mentioned in this book. With particular appreciation to Steve Hirst and the Sunshine Coast Daily for graciously allowing me to unleash all my words and publish them for the community each week. My praise to the team at radio Salt106.5 and listeners for their receptiveness to my enthusiasm to inspire dynamic relationships. To the experts in book world, publicist, Scott Eathorne and graphic designer, Joan Greenblatt and Ivona Angelovska who have patiently navigated me through unchartered territory. My appreciation to Ben Kingsley for inspiring this project to fruition along with brother, Chris Herrmann for his encouragement and logistic support and my enthusiastic preview readers. Special thanks to my amazing tribe of women including Megan Jantke, Kristin Lucas, Annemarie Hall, Tammy Hubycz and Liz Waters for their respective talents that gifted their unique perspective to this project.

I am grateful for all my teachers who include my parents, siblings and their relationships, university lecturers and particularly my perilous dating experiences prior to marriage!

To my past and future courageous clients proving their best beyond adversity, thank you for sharing your journeys at many of the most important junctures in life—I honour you.

HOW TO UNPACK THIS TOOLBOX

This book is your DIY Relationship Renovation manual. Just like any project you take on, read the instructions fully—I will help walk you through the process of using the major tools to support you in developing, renovating and maintaining a lasting, meaningful relationship. It becomes your easy reference guide for when challenges inevitably arise and some relationship maintenance is required. The Toolbox Topic titles are self-explanatory to easily locate your specific areas of need, however, don't overlook the self-evaluation at the start.

For those in the before, during or aftermath stages of a relationship, I hope that by having this book on your bedside table you will be able to enhance or transform your relationship skill set, propelling you towards love, care—and commitment, and particularly to strengthen your resolve to work through the tough times. Whilst it takes two to tango, you absolutely can read this solo and champion the change!

To quote one of my favourite authors, Mark Batterson, 'The right book in the right hands at the right time can save a marriage, avert a mistake, demand a decision, plant a seed, conceive a dream, solve a problem and prompt a prayer.'[1] I pray this book is one of them!

To complement this book, I've collated additional resources at www.relationshiprejuvenator.com to support you as you journey through renovating your relationship. It is never too late to begin.

INTRODUCTION

My great passion for relationship counselling comes from enabling every couple who walks through my door seeking positive change, to recreate and reform their legacy.

What would I know about this topic?

It seems I was destined to be an avid observer of relationships. As the fifth child in my family, the result of a complete surprise pregnancy (a 'whoopsie' is the technical term)—13 years after my siblings. I was brought up in the perfect environment to carefully examine, be mentored in and critique what good and bad relationships look like. Much like the natural historian, David Attenborough, I observed the fascinating primal dating habits of my siblings and their friends, as well as the marriage habits of my parents. As it turns out, my parents became the subject of town gossip that included suggestions that as a 38-year-old woman with four children, my Mum should terminate the pregnancy that resulted in me coming into the world. So, what I do know for sure is that I'm here to make a difference—inspiring couples to have the best relationships possible beyond the counselling room.

I was fortunate to be raised in what was ultimately a loving household that advocated discipline, a hard-work ethic and the benefits of contributing to the lives of others. Being the final product of more mature parents, there was little room for improvement in their—by then—very experienced parenting skills, which in turn left little room for testing their patience. In this home, I was exposed to the fantastic relationship mentoring of my Mum and Dad. They had been married 60 years by the time Dad passed away, exemplars for how love and the day-to-day organisation of a beautiful family unit could work. These were pretty high standards to live up to! So, by the time I was in my mid-30s, I decided despite all the dating I'd done, I wasn't prepared to settle for anything unless it was comparable to the positive and effective relationship of my parents. As many of you will know, sometimes we have to kiss a few frogs before we find our prince or princess.

I am a living, surviving testimony to heartbreak, rejection and loss. Those dating years sure were rough. I felt at times that I'd journeyed to the bottom of the well of male suitors and was left to claw myself out with regained self-confidence only to be excruciatingly splashed down again. It was lonely and daunting and I became increasingly full of self-doubt. At times it was nasty—enter the story of the boyfriend who suggested I had plastic surgery to my face. Imagine the shame, shock and myriad of painful emotions that followed that request? I was a ridiculously tall, blonde flight attendant already embroiled in the dreadful self-comparison with my glamorous crew 30,000 ft in the sky on a daily basis! Another nameless fellow gallantly picked me up to attend a disco, but left me there a few hours later after finding a better option. Then there were those I adored, but couldn't see a future with. My family even spent a month chewing up international phone cards whilst I wailed grief-stricken and heart-broken following a relationship break-up whilst living and studying in China!

My brothers coached me on the importance of checking for missing wedding bands. The key, they told me, is to look for indents on the ring finger and an absence of suntan in the same spot. They had to educate me so I would not fall prey to the deceitful married men who were looking for a fun night out! Whilst not to denigrate all pilots and Australian sports stars, some of the married ones I encountered were certainly brazen and gave insight into the world of potential infidelity.

Although certainly not at the time, I am now grateful for the harsh lessons learnt; the rollercoaster of experiences extreme enough to make the greatest thrill seeker choke, giving me empathy and insight to the distress and traumatic symptoms of my clients today.

My experience of grief and loss following a relationship break-up was not dissimilar to the sense of missing a limb. I, too, have inhaled a few too many packets of double-coated chocolate Tim Tams (the Australian version of indulgent goodness if you're not a local reader!) and spent multiple nights sobbing into my glass of wine or reluctantly having to put on a brave face and attend countless weddings. I vividly recall bawling throughout the entire car drive to a 70's themed hen's night wearing the most humungous black afro wig, reapplying my make-up in the car park on arrival, being surrounded by squealing joyful party-goers, and feeling sick, despondent and incredibly lonely on the inside.

I know first-hand the sense of failure and the toxic 'not good enough' self-talk that features all too frequently for the individuals and couples I work with today. I suspect I have only had a taste of what my clients experience, but I've had my decent share of time on the couch alone without an ounce of passion to dance when no-one was watching, let alone bother removing the black eye make-up from my chin.

I'm relieved I had the strength to not settle for a partner with inconsistent values to mine—for without it, I never would have met my perfect match. This also gives me firsthand experience of navigating life with someone who is not a clone of myself. I've been proudly married for 13 years and yes,

Relationships are mind-blowing, overwhelming, exciting, challenging, exhilarating, complicated, arousing, confusing, energising, problematical and often awkward.

we are normal: my husband does not seem to go about things the same way I do all the time and vice-versa—we do disagree! Together, we've learnt a healthy style of conflict observed by three active ('rambunctious' is the technical term) boys here on the Sunshine Coast in Queensland, Australia. We aim to emulate that same sense of respect, kindness and compassion for others displayed in the wonderful examples of our parents.

Our genuine love story of mutual adoration and respect is something I hope our boys will go on to recreate when they find partners. We have both been incredibly lucky to have had front-row seats to exemplary relationships despite challenges and disagreements. We all deserve to feel safe and know that there is nothing we can't attentively approach with our partners, even when the chips are down. Our respective parents weren't the only example of the high standards I hoped to achieve in my own relationship. Being an avid relationship observer, I noticed and loved the way my brother used his eyes to 'talk' with his wife of 30 years. This almost unconscious and intuitive observation has contributed significantly to my passion for relationships, and I, too, am living and breathing the experience of being in a relationship!

Relationships are mind-blowing, overwhelming, exciting, challenging, exhilarating, complicated, arousing, confusing, energising, problematical and often awkward. Why? Because no two people are alike. We are uniquely created and so are the incredible people we're attracted to.

We are ALL different! We ALL long to be loved, accepted and cherished. We all go about giving and getting the love we crave in our own special way. You may have 'nailed' a thriving and dynamic relationship, to find it in a dilapidated state just months or years later.

In a renovating sense, the term 'bonding' is the cementing action of an adhesive, such as glue. The opposite of adhesion is falling apart and severance. When you have TRI'ed Bonding—my revolutionary approach to managing conflict—and learnt to love with respect and kindness, you have a greater chance of a longer life, featuring the ability to take your health and happiness to greater heights.

I'm indebted to the couples I've seen over the years and throughout the book I describe selected stories in the general sense, disguising names and details for confidentiality. It is in their relationship renovation successes that I aspire to instil hope in you for *your* most important project.

My Renovation Journey

One of the earlier roles in my career was in corporate sales management in the airline industry. I handled all aspects of multiple large travel accounts, including taking calls from stressed-out businessmen who would call me from an airport such as in Singapore when something didn't go smoothly. My role was to stay calm, understand the problem, empathise and fix the situation. I remember thinking at the time *'I wonder what really happened to them in the lead up to this?'* Subsequently, as I moved closer to my passion which was always more community work, this was supported by flexible working hours as a flight attendant. Having been in the corporate sector for 12 years, I thought it would be a breath of fresh air. But again, I found myself dealing with very abusive, brash passengers and I would think, *'Wow! What happened to you?'* Believe it or not, not everyone riding in a plane is wonderfully happy to be jetting off to their next destination! This is where my interests in psychology and relationships began to take hold.

I began studying counselling part-time while I was still flying and also found time to continue volunteer work in rehabilitation centres, one of which was in Kings Cross, Sydney. It was here that those habits of observation came to the forefront again. Through simply paying attention to and helping people in crisis, making toasted sandwiches and cups of tea with ten sugars (preferred by those with drug addictions), I listened to how these people with troubled lives tried to cope with their relationships outside the centre. I came across university students working as prostitutes to pay their fees. I realised the importance of their close-knit community of friends which included ensuring their safety before, during and after client 'sessions'. They too relied on the importance of a debrief of their experiences for their mental health. I then went on to volunteer in a residential rehabilitation centre for women on the Sunshine Coast. Once again, I realised how the lack of a loving, constant and secure attachment with parents or caregivers can—but not always—carve the path for self-destructive behaviours, including self-harm and eating disorders.

Fast forward a few more years as more university counselling studies continued through my courtship, marriage and having children: it felt like every time I finished a semester, a baby turned up! Like most working mothers, the need to find a balance between nurturing my small children and contributing to the household, university practicum and my community was tricky. I began my private practice in general counselling with the support of my local church pastor who gladly welcomed my services in their office. Like most things we love and are truly destined for, the work, quite simply, found me.

Without consciously trying, I started attracting clients with relationship issues and became enraptured by this field of work! Some of my earliest clients were beautiful young couples with young children, who were desperate for positive change within themselves and their relationships. What completely blew me away, however, was that these young couples were not simply here to make *themselves* better. They were driven to become loving relationship mentors for their children, the kind my parents were for me. They wanted to draw a line in the sand and stop the cycle of separation/divorce/abuse/destruction they were trapped in. They wanted their legacy to be different. I thought, *Whoa! This is where we can impact generations.*

At this stage of my development as a counsellor, I had been married for six years and had three small children, which in itself was reassuring for my clients: I knew how hard it was to be married sometimes too! It's not easy all the time; I have learnt so much about relationships and to this day, I am often shocked when my husband doesn't agree with me or doesn't want the same things as me. That's called being in a relationship. Yes, initially conflict was tricky for us, we had to navigate a way of having differing opinions and ways of approaching differences healthily, especially when we transitioned into being 'married with children'. Our boys need to see us disagree and know that they're still safe and that it's still okay. That no one's leaving or slamming doors. That it's not a huge drama and life is normal.

Another normal is that if I've had a challenging day, my husband will inevitably be dealing with the flow on effect because that's part of being married. Have some children and watch that increase ten-fold! Pressures include having a sick child, being sick yourself at the same time and starting and running our own businesses. There were days when I'd had an hour's sleep and had been crying my eyes out and just couldn't think straight—how on earth can you be expected to get along with your partner at the same time? And that's where we are simply human because my husband and I are not always the best version of ourselves in those moments. What we find essential is ensuring that we align ourselves by constantly evaluating how we do things—from our expectations of the children's age-appropriate chores and our planning of disciplinary consequences through to how we roll as a couple.

Introduction

Part of my pre-marriage education for couples involves gently gifting those starry-eyed, loved up couples with my vast experience of working with high conflict couples. I systematically highlight many of the challenges they confront: your partner may come home grumpy, or you might not have the same libido as them at certain times (or any time!) and you might not have the same focus or goals at different stages of your relationship. My husband met me as a flight attendant with long blonde hair and now he's married to a marriage therapist with short hair of varying colours depending on the week—he didn't get exactly what he signed up for! In spite of this evolution, we still desire each other and love making it work. Life changes…how do you cope when yours does?

People give up on their marriage for many different reasons and many don't realise how much the legacy we are handed impacts our current relationships. It doesn't mean that because your parents separated, you will. It doesn't mean that because a parent was an alcoholic that you will automatically become one. I see this in couples again and again, as we talk about how we form habits like alcoholism, separation and divorce that have a tendency to flow through generations. Often those people might say, 'I don't drink because my Dad was an alcoholic' or 'My parents separated and that means that I never will.' It doesn't always work like that as these are themes which are often repeated; unfortunately, these couples have to work a lot harder because in their sub-conscious mind it *is* an option to just opt-out.

There will be times when your house will be rocked more than you feel you can handle. If you're suffering from abuse in any form, I urgently ask you to bravely talk to a trusted friend, family member or seek out the help of a professional relationship counsellor because we are designed to rely on others and sometimes need help to realise the kind of love we deserve. An unsafe environment is an unacceptable legacy you want to avoid, particularly where children are involved. You were designed to be loved and cherished.

My great passion for relationship counselling comes from enabling every couple who walks through my door seeking positive change, to recreate and reform their legacy. Rather than opting-out, we can instead work towards breaking some well-rehearsed, but unhelpful relationship habits. This is where my incredibly simple conflict resolution concept, TRI Bonding comes in. The diagram I have developed to demonstrate this concept is based on the triangle—the strongest of all geometric shapes. It simply demonstrates how you can easily navigate most of your relationship challenges by considering the three elements in my TRI Bonding philosophy.

Some of my most beautiful opportunities arise when clients with legacies of separation, divorce and all sorts of abuse come with open hearts and minds to say, 'We don't like how we were raised; we didn't get to see how beautiful marriage and family can be. Can you please give us strategies so that we don't leave the same legacy? Could you please help us help our children?' Oh my gosh! I get goose bumps thinking about the exciting potential of flourishing and dynamic relationships for those beautiful children, most of whom I will likely never meet.

Let me support you in rejuvenating your relationship for a lifetime of unbridled passion, unwavering admiration, steadfast love and respect. I've been training for my job my entire life and have spent way too many hours pursuing my passion of researching, writing a weekly column and curating excellent resources for dynamic and thriving relationships to simply leave them gathering digital and actual dust on my computer and bookshelf.

Love is a temporary madness, it erupts like volcanoes and then subsides. And when it subsides you have to make a decision. You have to work out whether your roots have so entwined together that it is inconceivable that you should ever part. Because this is what love is.

Love is not breathlessness, it is not excitement, it is not the promulgation of promises of eternal passion. That is just being in love, which any fool can do. Love itself is what is left over when being in love has burned away, and this is both an art and a fortunate accident.

Those that truly love have roots that grow towards each other underground, and when all the pretty blossoms have fallen from their branches, they find that they are one tree and not two.

—Louis de Bernières, *Captain Corelli's Mandolin*

Renovate Your Relationship

ABOUT LOVE

Find health and happiness by actively seeking opportunities to give and support others in your daily life and the joy will follow: science proves it!

What Is love?

Laura is an envied woman you'd be certain to admire across a café. Donned in an expensive suit, with glossy pulled-back hair crowning her gorgeous face she exudes confidence that speaks of prosperity. But behind those pricey dark sunglasses are eyes that reflect a deep sadness and anguish.

Laura was raised amongst a large, chaotic family of four siblings. Her upper middle class, well-educated parents had sufficient money, a nice home and regular enviable holidays accompanied by the young nanny of the month. Despite repeated early attempts until the age of around seven, she made a decision she could not count on her argumentative, sometimes violent and inattentive parents for support. There were significant moments in time when she longed for consolation and attention. She was rebuffed by either their physical absence on work trips, dismissed as a distraction to their next urgent report to write, or ignored because they were recovering from their late-night alcohol-fuelled quarrels—it was futile. As the nannies came and went, school was a less volatile environment and books became her escape. They allowed Laura to circumvent the pain of feeling isolated and unloved at home.

As an astute and independent young woman, Laura went on to graduate from law, strove for perfection at many levels in academia and pursued adventure through travelling the world. Despite these successes, she had a trail of failed romantic relationships as a result of having conditioned herself to avoid relying on others. Those suitors struggled to connect with her at a deeper level as she withdrew when her feelings of love became too intimate. Laura enjoyed worldly success but throughout her extended years of living alone in a swanky apartment in Sydney she continued keeping people at 'arms-length'. She subsequently suffered bouts of dysfunctional eating, swinging between weight gain, bulimia and depression and all the while managing to hold onto her career where her colleagues were oblivious to her struggles.

By age thirty-five, Laura succumbed to the deep blue eyes of a dapper, fine fellow, Brad. They met at a conference and he was equally successful and had perfectly matched intelligence to challenge and excite her. He was attentive, caring and made her feel special like she had never experienced before.

I first met Laura when she was seeking couples therapy with Brad whom she had married five years earlier. Now with three young children, they were fast spiralling into the patterns of their separate (though similar) disconnected pasts and sought to overcome repeated conflict amongst the stress of their work commitments and parenting. They were desperate, hostile and on the brink of moving into their own apartments; they had the usual long journey of grieving and emotional deregulation ahead of them as they prepared to forge the unhappy path to divorce. It is these scenarios where breaking the 'shackles' of patterns of history can impact future generations.

No matter how compromised your home life was as a child, how much you're grieving from loss, how bullied you've been, or how neglected, lonely or subsequently depressed you feel—finding someone to provide you emotional attentiveness can be your turning point toward thriving and joy. Enjoying a long-term, trusting, therapeutic alliance with another beautiful human who will listen, guide and support your choice to grow is a gift. Those people who help you realise you truly matter are paramount.

One reason I passionately pursue my work of inspiring as many relationships as possible in our community is the reality of how many Australians are suffering from either depression or anxiety. This was highlighted during my breakfast radio interview with sociologist, psychologist and social researcher Hugh Mackay, who says we need to be increasingly aware of the silent sufferers in the 'grip of our mental health crisis'. Add social distancing throughout a pandemic and we are catapulted toward an urgent evaluation of how we live and care for others.

Dr Mackay quotes Beyond Blue in saying that 'two million Australians are suffering from a diagnosed anxiety disorder'. One major theme is his observation of our socially-fragmented society, which is more evident now than at any previous time in our history. Why are our relationships in the community suffering?

- Our household numbers are shrinking. One in four households has one person living in it and this looks to increase to one in three in the near future.
- 35% to 40% of marriages end in divorce, which has a massive ripple effect on society and subsequent generations, including children who transition between their parents' houses or choose to live independently earlier.
- The decreasing birth rate (those with children know that we are 'forced' to socialise through extracurricular activities, visits with their friends, school events or just by being with them playing in the street.)
- We compensate with pets!
- We're more mobile and move homes on average every six years.
- Busyness seems to be our badge of honour.
- Dr Mackay says the information technology boom, 'makes us feel more connected than ever before'. On the other hand, it makes it easier than ever for us to stay apart from each other and to settle for a text or a tweet, rather than a phone call, let alone a cup of coffee. We are getting used to the idea that you can communicate without human presence.

There are a lot of folk I know living alone who love hogging the television remote. Whilst they can enjoy such benefits as being able to leave as many dishes in the sink as they like, for as long as they like, many do experience significant loneliness.

Loneliness is said to be in the top three social challenges facing Australia. We are created relationally; humans are social beings.

When we feel loved, secure and attached to people and our surroundings, we flourish. Look beyond the real symptoms of anxiety and you'll see the social fragmentation behind it. In my experience, loneliness and disconnection are usually the root cause of addictions too.

Dr Mackay highlighted the astounding results of the Compassionate Frome project.[2] Frome Medical Practice, serving the 28,000 strong population of Frome, Somerset in the United Kingdom, took the innovative approach of combining a compassionate program of community development with routine medical care. They reduced emergency admissions to hospital by 30% over three years! What was their secret antidote? They make standard use of the most effective intervention for improving health and longevity—social relationships! They recognise social connectedness has a bigger impact on health than giving up smoking, reducing excessive drinking, reducing obesity or any other preventative interventions.

> We are created relationally; humans are social beings. When we feel loved, secure and attached to people and our surroundings, we flourish.

Compassionate Communities, UK notes, 'Until now, it has not been known how to use this in routine clinical practice.' They managed to reconnect people to their support network and to the extensive community activity that already exists. They recognise that they don't seek to take the place of social care, but use this methodology:

- Taking advantage of supportive networks of family, friends and neighbours and the sense of belonging that provides

care, connection, love, laughter and companionship.
- Building networks of support for the routine matters of life: shopping, cooking, cleaning, looking after the garden and pets, providing transport.
- Linking to community activity such as choirs, walking groups, men's sheds, talking cafes and other interest groups where people can make friendships and share life events.

Together, compassionate communities help to reduce isolation and loneliness and bring a sense of belonging into what is sometimes a disconnected society.

Furthermore, Mackay says, 'For too long now, we have been living in a society that revolves around individualism and consumerism.' He calls them the 'twin vanities.' Hugh emphasises this in what he calls being entangled in the QPL syndrome: The Quest for the Perfect Latte. He says our sense of lack of control in the world causes us to seek fulfilment through bathroom renovations, breast implants, enviable holidays we can Instagram and demands for the perfect latte. We are ensnared in the false belief we will be happy when we get what we think we deserve. In reality, it is a never-ending chasm to fill and the root of entitlement and narcissism. Mackay says we have 'lost sight of our true nature as people who belong to a society. We are, each of us, organically linked to the whole; its problems

> So as relationally designed humans, most of us long to be connected to a significant other, to matter. The incredulous, heady rush of being valued and cherished is the mind-blowing part that songs are made of.

are our problems; the pain of any is the pain of all.'

Whilst you might not be able to claim your cup of coffee after choir practice on your healthcare fund, why not chat to that person behind the counter at the store or at the airport and be bold enough to make a connection? This is what truly matters and ultimately you may save someone's life because you extended a smile, some warmth and kindness.

So as relationally designed humans, most of us long to be connected to a significant other, to matter. The incredulous, heady rush of being valued and cherished is the mind-blowing part that songs are made of.

This is love.

But for many of us, myself included, finding the right kind of love from the right person and then making a commitment to always nurture that love is hardly ever a smooth process—even when you think you've found 'the one'. As much as it can be heartbreaking, dating helps to work out what you do and don't want in a partner. Sometimes it's a complete misalignment in values, perhaps the creeping in of abuse or maybe just a lack of passion for one another that causes a relationship to come to an end. I know from experience how hard it can be to walk away from someone. Sadly, I had to discontinue a relationship with a perfectly kind and suitable partner. Everything seemed fine, except there was no feeling of '*Oh my gosh! I won't be able to breathe if I don't spend the rest of my life with this person!*' On another level, our core values also weren't in alignment.

Unfortunately, the immediacy of our 'now' society means we expect an instant, fast connection and a quick fix to everything. I'm talking about the next Netflix episode 'coming up' in eight seconds, high speed online information, fast food and a pill for everything else—life is fast in the 21st century. Our ability to heal, change and develop positive relationships is time-consuming but ultimately, we must consciously change. I'm wondering how post-pandemic times might re-align our values here.

Gone are the days you can blame your inherited genes for all your shonky habits, depression, anxiety or even a tendency to chew with your mouth open. Sorry folks, according to Dr John Arden, author of *Mind-Brain-Gene: Toward Psychotherapy Integration*,[3] you can only allocate two per cent of your 'pre-determined' genes to that. The

> Genes only lay out potentials and vulnerabilities, but don't dictate your thoughts, feelings or behaviour.

rest are non-encoded, which means the other 98% is affected by your environment and subsequently, your ability to self-regulate, apply self-discipline and be resilient in the face of adversity. Genes only lay out potentials and vulnerabilities, but don't dictate your thoughts, feelings or behaviour. This is so important to realise, especially for couples who feel like their inevitable separation has been predetermined by their parent's legacy of divorce.

Even the smallest of mammals show that nurturing others with your love leads to greater happiness. Research proves that rat pups that were lovingly licked by their rat mummy have greater resilience and regulation than those who didn't enjoy such a caring environment.[4] These happy little gnarly rodents enjoy a more effective thermostat for stress featuring less cortisol and more serotonin (the happy neurojuice). Dr Arden says that we can adjust those 98% of non-encoded genes by changing our responses, behaviour and environment! Change that and your brain changes. Very cool.

Love is the answer. Despite adversity from those raised in a 'compromised background,' you can turn down your 'antennae' which may be on high alert for feeling hurt or for danger from the risk of loving another human again. Learn to approach life versus avoiding it and enjoy great relationships. This is when happiness flows!

If you're currently in a relationship and feeling bogged down in it, consider getting out of that vehicle of contemplating separation or divorce as a potential solution. Instead, lead the relationship positively and proactively. You can then have some peace of mind knowing that you at least gave the relationship 100% before you chose which road to take.

Love on the Brain

You've got to love the fabulous and prolific research about the brain, and specifically, about joy and fulfilment! Neuroscience research shows that a specific pattern of brain activity occurs when you perform kind acts for others.[5] This is why your parents asked you to play nicely!

If you were to hand over $100 to someone in need without expecting anything in return, the limbic region of your brain will go *bing*! Okay, so it won't make that sound, but it'll reflect the significance of your compassionate activity. Furthermore, your medial prefrontal cortex and temporoparietal junction would also very likely want to say something like, *'Nice one!'* if they could.

There was also a very cool study published in *Science*, conducted through the University of Oregon about neuroarchitecture and altruism.[6] They proved when their research subjects donated money both voluntarily or involuntarily, the part of the brain associated with processing unexpected rewards became active. The neurons there secrete dopamine, a neurotransmitter that plays a key role in reward-motivated behaviour (you also get a hit of this with 'likes' on your Instagram post). The team found higher amounts of dopamine were secreted for each subject when voluntarily choosing to donate as opposed to when they were forced to.

As it turns out, whether we expect a reward or not, the midbrain will become activated regardless of whether we are sad or happy with our reason for doing it. It's interesting that, whether you feel good about it is irrelevant to this 'hardwired' reward activity. Whilst there's much to be explored in this field, you can't ignore these findings about the warm fuzzies your brain and body experience when you're benevolent!

> There sure is a time to grieve and be sad, but one wonderful strategy to move beyond that time is finding the greatest fulfilment in what I believe is inherent in our human design–serving others. Even YOU have unique talents waiting to be gifted to others.

We know that the brain changes according to experience. Activities like focusing, contemplating and giving cause it to grow and change. This is consistent with evidence that your genes can be affected by your own environment. It makes absolute sense that you can practise and train yourself or your children to be gracious and helpful for health reasons.

Find health and happiness by actively seeking opportunities to give and support others in your daily life and the joy will follow: the science above proves it! If you have children, create rituals in your family that inspire regular contributing together, allowing the act of 'giving' to become a natural and enjoyable part of their culture from a young age.

Even if you believe you're going through a rough patch or you are feeling unattractive, on the outer, like a failure or lonely, the simple act of giving to or helping out someone else—your partner perhaps—is an excellent way to support anyone experiencing a bad day, including yourself.

You may have read the beautiful poem about seasons from Ecclesiastes 3: 1-8 that says, *'There's a time to break down, and a time to build up; A time to weep, and a time to laugh; a time to mourn, and a time to dance; A time to cast away stones, and a time to gather stones together; a time to embrace, and a time to refrain from embracing; A time to get, and a time to lose; a time to keep, and a time to cast away; A time to rend, and a time to sew; a time to keep silence, and a time to speak...'*

Is this your worst time? Take even the smallest step to turn toward someone else and you can turn your shocking time into your best time by gifting a service to someone. There sure is a time to grieve and be sad, but one wonderful strategy to move beyond that time is finding the greatest fulfilment in what I believe is inherent in our human design–serving others. Even YOU have unique talents waiting to be gifted to others. A neighbour, a stranger or an organisation will be forever grateful for the day you choose to turn your own atrocious, depressing day into your best.

Surprise someone in your street with a home-made yummy something, pay for someone's coffee anonymously, deliver food hampers, work at the soup kitchen, create, craft or build anything required. If you aren't motivated yet, take a look at these reasons why you will benefit—serving others also offers the chance to:

- act on your values, passions and interests
- make new friendships and create professional networks
- gain work experience and learn new skills
- enjoy new social and cultural experiences
- develop personally and build confidence
- enjoy better physical and mental health (studies show volunteering makes us healthier and happier)
- challenge yourself in a supportive environment
- help your community
- have fun!

Think of the iconic Oprah Winfrey. She had a truly tough life as a young woman and she turned it all around by *giving* to others. Another gob-smacking example is Nick Vujicic, born in 1982 in Melbourne, Australia without arms and legs and with no medical explanation or reason why. Imagine going through your day without hands or legs? Despite the obvious struggle, he refused to allow this to inhibit his lifestyle. Now married with children, he travels the world speaking to diverse groups.

Then there's another Australian icon, Turia Pitt, who in 2011 at the age of 24, suffered full-thickness burns to 65% of her body whilst competing in a 100km ultra-marathon in the Australian outback. She encountered an out-of-control grass fire, was trapped by the blaze and was not expected to survive when she was choppered out of the remote desert. Turia lost seven fingers, spent over six months in hospital, underwent more than 200 operations and spent two years in recovery.

Fast forward a few years and she subsequently competed in her first Ironman competition followed by the Ironman World Championships in Kona, Hawaii. Over the years, Turia has written a number of books, been honoured with multiple awards, mentored thousands of people to achieve their greatest goals through her online programs and joined one of her heroes, Tony Robbins, as a headline speaker at the 2018 National Achievers Congress. Pretty impressive accolades for someone who was told she wouldn't ever walk, run or be independent again.

You don't have to be an international superstar or motivational speaker to have an impact. I have heard countless stories of incredible people from diverse socio-economic backgrounds—including those that enter my counselling room—who continue to make the world of difference all because they had a shocker. I spent twelve sessions with John, an incredible and kind-hearted road construction worker raised by alcoholic parents. He suffered tremendously from witnessing his brother's tragic suicide and the subsequent trauma that affected his emotional presence in his marriage and children. Together we re-constructed helpful new nurturing thoughts to make clarity toward reconnection, hope and a strengthened marriage. There was the incredibly talented country and western singer I journeyed with from childhood neglect, who is now sky-rocketing to musical success, and the high performing medical specialist recovering from his relationship breakdown and depression who found new love and international medical research accolades.

No one is immune to adversity and as long as you're breathing, everyone has an opportunity to choose not to allow adversity to consume you. Consume *it* by making a world of difference and taking one step closer to your time to dance. For some of us, the idea of helping others is so much easier than giving love and care to those you are closest to, even married to. Imagine what would happen if you helped your marriage in the same way? The giving of flowers has become a symbol of apology, but imagine what it would do if they were simply 'because I love you' flowers? Think of the way your brain would light up; think of how your partner's would!

> No one is immune to adversity and as long as you're breathing, everyone has an opportunity to choose not to allow adversity to consume you.

Take a moment to examine yourself though— you may have become addicted to lighting up your brain in unhealthy ways. Social media could be one of them. My husband and I both use our screens like many people—for entertainment, for recipes, for the footy scores, for planning our children's social calendars—but we have to make sure it's constantly monitored so that we don't lose ourselves in our separate zones on our screens.

We can also get tunnel vision with our robotic and urgent to-do's, become stuck in the latest reality television series or be so distracted by our own problems that we lose sight of this grand beautiful picture standing right in front of us! We can lose sight of the possibilities of a world where we stay true to our inherent design of relying on and enjoying dynamic relationships. I believe the 2020 pandemic has reminded us of the importance to stop and remember this.

Marriage—What's the Point?

So if all this love and caring and being nice is so helpful in making us feel better, why is marriage such an important piece of the relationship puzzle? Why get married at all? Quite simply, the physical, psychological, emotional, social and financial benefits of stable, loving relationships for men, women, children and even society in general, are overwhelming.

The Institute of Family Studies[7] revealed that married people enjoy better mental health for the life of the family unit. Furthermore, parents around the globe who want their children to enjoy the benefits of a stable childhood should marry rather than cohabit. The IFS report[8] found that children whose parents were living together, but not married at the time of their birth are, by aged 12, much more likely to see their parents split. Even in those countries where cohabitation has become culturally acceptable, it is found to be a much more fragile union than marriage.

Wendy Manning's research paper *Cohabitation and Child Wellbeing*, shows that statistically, couples who marry stay together longer, providing stability for their children.[9] The very nature of hosting a wedding and the very public display of commitment that comes with it, grants greater meaning and intention to bond for life. For those who assign religious meaning to their marriage as well, this transition can allow the couple to deepen their bonds with each other, as well as help them form a deeper relationship with God.

In a household with two parents, children have more balanced perspective observing two different role models, whilst also benefitting from receiving twice as much emotional and practical support while growing up. The long-term result of this is well-balanced children who are less inclined to turn to problematic behaviours as they become older. For boys, they are less likely to display delinquent behaviour and indulge in substance abuse as they grow older and for girls, they are less likely to be promiscuous.[10] Regardless of whether you have children or not, monogamy in marriage reduces sexually transmitted diseases and leads to an even more fulfilling sex life as couples grow in their knowledge of their respective desires and can work towards satisfying them based on trust.

> Being married also means that you are a united force to be reckoned with. You can draw on your respective skills to become a highly functioning team that you would not have been on your own ...

Being married also means that you are a united force to be reckoned with. You can draw on your respective skills to become a highly functioning team that you would not have been on your own—or at least bolster up what the other is not so fantastic at. I always laugh at the fact that my husband can pack the boot of the car way quicker and better than I could ever get my head around. On the other hand, I am a very nurturing person, while my husband's lack of empathy is legendary. I quite literally have to say, 'Ben—I've got a cold, this is where you ask me if I'm okay and do I need anything?' Thankfully he has other wonderful talents!

It is also common knowledge (I'm finding it difficult to locate a reliable source on this one, but we all know it to be true) that women are naturally gifted with a higher visual perceptiveness in many situations. Accordingly, marriage brings lifelong support for a man trying to find his wallet and keys. In return, many women may choose to benefit from the time saved shaving their legs once that ring is on. There's an unlimited 'Get Out of XYZ' pass, like the oft used, 'My husband is dreadfully sick so I can't make it to the (incredibly boring) office party'. Married people can negotiate on a life plan that allows them to share and/or offload the home duties they loathe. A long-term committed marriage can also lead to intimate gestures such as the armpit sniff test, pimple squeezing and checking for nits.

Of course, there is also the bonus that your swiping finger for Tinder can be used for other more beneficial tasks and you no longer have to worry about which way to swipe. There's no doubt that your partner keeps you alive by reminding you in the gentlest of ways what you're not so good at… such as buying that too-big-for-you motorbike or attending the Spanish tomato throwing festival when you're allergic to tomatoes!

There are often financial benefits and other associated simplicities associated with insurances, organising inheritances for your children and the like, along with a myriad number of emotional benefits. But all jokes aside, those in a committed marriage have greater emotional wellbeing as a result of being able to share the stresses of daily life

You'll recall Laura and Brad's mental distress, loneliness and subsequent fast-track to the brink of separation. They were unable to take the risk to be vulnerable to share their inner world resulting in being ill-equipped for navigating conflict. They experienced the common strain of sleepless nights with young children as well as unintentionally mimicking their parents' similar legacy of a frantic and volatile communication style; with these contributing factors it seems they were destined to see their relationship fail.

I was privileged to guide and bear witness to their determination and tenacity resulting in an inspiring and united approach to changing that future using the tools in this book—to support them in breaking free from the patterns of behaviour that had governed their relationship thus far. Their new approach features vulnerability and intimacy and is now a harmonious legacy from which their equally intelligent pre-teens can model their own relationships—knowing that the solid foundation of a great relationship is imperative for their own well-being. My strategy to their successful journey for that flourishing and dynamic connection starts in the next toolbox topic.

Love is a necessary and natural part of our lives. Without it, we are miserable. With it, we are joyful, feel valued and well-loved. From the personal experience of those nebulous feel-good feelings to the hard-scientific facts presented from a stream of studies and experiments, we all agree we need love. However, the search for that partner who will stand by you in a long term and committed relationship, perhaps most effectively in the form of marriage, is not always easy. But once you have found them, it is time to give them the best of yourself.

TAKEAWAY TOOLS

For some, that 'I love you so much I can't breathe' momentum gradually subsides as time goes on and children and challenges accumulate over the years, but it's not time to give up or dip out!

Marriage is not an ancient and outdated tradition: it is a wonderful celebration of the love you have for your partner. It shows the commitment you have to your relationship for life and comes with a host of feel-good benefits not just for you, but for those around you and especially any children you produce along the way!

- Work out what you want in a life partner and/or what it was that attracted you to yours in the first place.
- Love is a necessary part of life: it is a scientifically proven fact that we flourish on connection.
- The act of receiving and giving love, lights up your brain far more authentically than any clever Instagram or Facebook post.

Renovate Your Relationship

LOOK IN THE MIRROR

The light bulb goes on when we do a self-evaluation to have a look at exactly what practices we are contributing to the relationship, from a list of those that support great relationships.

When couples first present themselves in my counselling sessions, the 'Blame Game' is generally in full swing, with each partner seeking to find someone impartial to tell how the other is so awful to live with. It's a huge theme running throughout my sessions. For those invested in the Blame Game, they are usually a little disappointed when I gently and compassionately point their outstretched finger back towards themselves. The light bulb goes on when we do a self-evaluation to have a look at exactly what practices we are contributing to the relationship, from a list of those that support great relationships.

It's easy to play the Blame Game with our partners; to lay the fault of a failing relationship at their feet and in their inability to do the little or big things like picking up their dirty underpants off the floor or saying hello with love in their eyes as they walk in after work. Yet quite often, we don't bother or see fit to turn that focus on ourselves.

Let me give you an example. If your self-esteem is low when you first meet your life partner, he or she might be wonderfully reassuring, saying things like, 'You're great!' or 'I love how you do that!' You might counter with, 'No, I'm not good at this, I'm just not worth it.' All those beautiful 'can't-breathe-without-you' feelings will naturally inspire more reassure, 'Yes you are! I love you! You're amazing!'

It's unreasonable to think that your partner will (or even should) be able to keep up that kind of reassurance for 60, or even 10 years. It becomes exhausting and sooner or later the partner will begin to ignore the behaviour, throw their hands up and say 'You know what? I can't do this anymore.' It's at this point that you might wallow in further despair, before deciding that your partner is an uncaring narcissist. What happened? You dropped the ball on being the best version of yourself and leant rather unfairly on your partner to 'complete' you. In a loving, caring and effective relationship, partners complement—rather than complete—each other.

> Taking responsibility for being the best version of yourself in your relationship is paramount in creating and maintaining a healthy, loving marriage. And believe me, identifying your faults and then working through them is not like opening up a big bag of sunshine and lollipops.

Taking responsibility for being the best version of yourself in your relationship is paramount in creating and maintaining a healthy, loving marriage. And believe me, identifying your faults and then working through them is not like opening up a big bag of sunshine and lollipops. I can descend into tears easily when I'm tired and know I'm not perfect. Neither is my husband and we *all* make mistakes on an almost daily basis. But it is *my* responsibility to stay fit, it is *my* responsibility to look after my mental health and it is *my* responsibility to be the best version of me. Only in this way do I truly contribute to my relationship in a meaningful way that will support its longevity. Challenges will come up from outside your relationship; you might lose your job, become seriously ill or lose a loved one. That's when partners support each other—through those tough times.

I'll often require each partner to rate themselves between one and ten on an array of relational topics. They might rate themselves as a ten at greeting their partner warmly when they get home every day. It's at this point the conversation opens up, with one admitting, 'Well, actually I know that I should greet my partner warmly, but because he pisses me off so much, I don't do it.' I might ask the couple how often they compliment each other using eye contact, with the response ranging from, 'I used to' to 'I never have' to 'Am I supposed to do that?'

Most couples get a bit of a jolt by going through this process; it can be a little depressing to see how far they've drifted from that loving relationship they began with. I typically reassure them, 'Hey, by the time people courageously arrive in my office, they're probably not going to rate themselves very highly.' It's not a test where I can add up all of the results and rate people as good or bad. This exercise is aimed at developing insight and realising that blaming the other person for the current failings within the relationship is unhelpful at best, and nasty at worst.

Taking a look at whether each partner is presenting the best version of themselves to each other or whether they are stuck in a cycle of stress, resentment and unforgiveness is a major step in gaining insight into how that couple might have arrived in front of me in the first place. You can enjoy that self-evaluation quiz at www.relationshiprejuvenator.com/self-evaluation to ensure you get a head start.

Earlier, I mentioned the incredible Turia Pitt who has not only achieved great sporting success, but is now juggling a demanding career as a married woman with children. We aired one her video clips featured on social media on our morning radio show. It shared her

> '...when we expect and demand so much from one person, of course we're going to be let down because no one is perfect.'

best relationship advice which is quite simply to, 'Drop your expectations!'. She went on to say, 'Now I know that sounds counterintuitive, but when we expect and demand so much from one person, of course, we're going to be let down because no one is perfect. Not you, not me, not your partner...not anyone. And your partner can't be your business coach, the person you have deep and meaningful conversations with, your adventure buddy, perfect with money, but very generous at the same time, and also make heaps of cash and they're clean and tidy and a great cook and handy around the house and super sexy and serenade you with a guitar and heaps of you know, laughs and wants to spend a lot of time with you, but is also really popular and has an amazing group of friends and picks their towels up off the floor and they're never in a bad mood. You know all those things, all at once, I think it's unrealistic. So, this list of staggering expectations, in my opinion, is way too much for one person to fulfil. Because if I'm being honest, I know that I'm not perfect and I don't have such high standards and so for me to expect such high standards from someone else I think would be a bit unfair.'

Nurturing the Best Version of Yourself

In this crazy 'first world', it seems we unquestionably need the latest groovy gadgets to feel a sense of worthiness. Have you seen that smart fridge where you don't need to open the door to see what's inside? It also communicates with your grocery store if something is missing—I so need that! Or is it more that *I want* it? Many of us are striving to keep up with Instagram-worthy exotic holidays or the idyllic Facebook lives we see, or maybe we're eating way too much, yet drowning in guilt for being too exhausted to get to the gym. Inevitably, you find yourself working like crazy to haul in the required cash for this enviable lifestyle and mulling over all the things you're not. Is this the person your partner fell in love with?

You can't enjoy dynamic and flourishing relationships if you're the withdrawn shadow of your former exuberant self. When you can't contribute to your intimate partner, family and friends because you're so exhausted, sad, depressed or full of self-loathing; very few of your interactions with them will end positively. Investing in the best version of yourself is not a narcissistic exercise in doing whatever you want, but rather a lifelong process of nurturing your strengths and improving on your weaknesses. In the long run, you'll simply feel happier about yourself and once that happens, you can begin to see the joy return to your relationship as well. I am perpetually in awe of the vulnerability and openness of clients who enthusiastically approach the notion of evaluating and renewing their mind following adversity—it can be transformational! The wonderful bonus for couples I meet experiencing relationship dissatisfaction, is the personal growth they individually achieve in their progress toward reconnection. One tool that can complement this process is the Johari Window.[11] It is designed to inspire self-awareness by representing your feelings, experiences, views, attitudes, skills and motivation etc. from four perspectives. You can view and complete my version at www.relationshiprejuvenator.com/jwindow.

For some who are far down the deep, dark relationship well, simply 'feeling happier' to improve upon their relationship seems like a catch 22—an immense and difficult task with mutually dependent conditions. Becoming the best version of you is achievable, though—beginning with small changes, completed frequently.

I had the honour of interviewing US neuropsychologist Dr John Arden at an International Association of Applied Neuroscience conference. Dr Arden has devised the handy acronym SEEDS to help you transform your brain, body and soul from sluggish and depressed to happy and healthy. Designed to keep your relationships thriving, as well as to beat off depression and anxiety, this acronym is worth placing in a prominent spot (perhaps on your bathroom mirror) for a constant reminder of how you can easily live a more fulfilling lifestyle.

> **S - Social Connectivity**: I know it can get so 'peopley' out there sometimes, but like it or not, we are designed relationally and thrive on emotional attentiveness. Loneliness causes cellular changes resulting in a weakened immune system, a propensity for addiction and even early symptoms of dementia. Our telomeres (caps on the end of our chromosomes) can shrink without cultivated and fostered social brain networks. Keep yourself engaged with real-time authentic family (like

your partner) or friends, rather than online acquaintances, likers and followers.

E - Exercise: Dr Arden says exercise is better than any anti-depressant or anxiety tool on the planet! He encourages 30 minutes of increased heart rate activity each day to stave off the blues. An array of awesome brain-enhancing biochemical processes occurs when we exercise, which includes producing new neurons in our brain (no wonder all my best ideas are invented during a long jog, though I'm unsure about the proven science of all my other 'shower-inspired' fabulous new theories!).

E - Education: Have you heard the saying, 'If you don't use it, you lose it'? True story. If you're not constantly learning, you're not building an infrastructure of brain connectivity. The more connectivity, the richer your cognitive reserve later in life. Yale Professor Paul Bloom specialises in cognitive psychology and pleasure research. He says pleasure doesn't just occur; it develops.[12] Want to know how to get it? He says study more! Aside from the frequently confirmed knowledge that a headache will result from guzzling a lot of expensive wine, why not increase your pleasure and happiness in fermented grapes by learning more about it on the way? Instead of seeking delight from experiencing something over and over, gain knowledge about your object of pleasure as well.

D - Diet: Feed your brain with nutritious fuel because your brain chemicals need it to function well. A diet of deep-fried hot chips and sauce will starve your amazingly created head of healthy neurotransmitters. Poor food choices inhibit clear and positive thinking.

Neuroscientist Dr Caroline Leaf states that 95% of your serotonin (a natural mood-stabilising chemical produced by your nerve cells) and half of the dopamine transmitters (your chemical messengers) are produced in your gut, so putting healthy, fresh and nourishing things in there is a no-brainer.[13]

Furthermore, don't fall into the trap of eating on the go. Eat slowly until you're 80% full and let your mind be your guide—not your eyes! Dr Leaf quotes this mind-blowing research: '75 to 98% of current mental, physical, emotional, and behavioural illnesses and issues stem from our thought life; only 2 to 25% come from a combination of genetics and what enters our bodies through food, medications, pollution, chemicals and so on.'[14] This illustrates the incredible impact of eating habits behind a healthy mindset.

S - Sleep: Achieving functional sleep is a deterrent for depression and anxiety. Dr Arden says sleep medications can hinder our sleep cycle, which is required to naturally consolidate memories. Your brain and body stay quite active during sleep when they join forces in a housekeeping-type role to remove toxins. When we mess it all up with drugs and alcohol, it makes sense that we experience that very apt term I recently heard—'hangxiety'—and the corresponding dreadful symptoms afterwards. Do it often enough and you get depressed and anxious. Struggling in this area? Start with mindfulness, prayer, exercise or a therapist to collaborate on sleep strategies to combat over-thinking at all the wrong times.

Planting fruitful SEEDS for your relationship begins with being the best version of yourself. Once you have begun to master each area, the benefits to your body, your mind and your relationships will be obvious. Mastering SEEDS is not the final destination on the journey to a happy life; that journey never ends. Maintaining that loving, joyful version of you is the other very important element of happiness within your relationships.

> Your whirring toxic thoughts of can't and not good enough will continue to hold you in a vice-like grip if you allow your brain to be stuck in the comfort of your discomfort.

The following are further ideas to make sure you are constantly investing in the best version of yourself for great relationships:

- **The comfort of your discomfort**
  Your whirring toxic thoughts of can't and not good enough will continue to hold you in a vice-like grip if you allow your brain to be stuck in the comfort of your discomfort. It sure is a familiar, cosy place, but only you control your thoughts. You are the only one who can harness control of your mind and body and choose to change and evolve.

- **Stop looking for shortcuts**
  Sorry to break it to you, but those abs really won't reveal themselves with a pill. Your glowing skin won't shine while

you eat hot pies slathered in sauce and your dream job won't be offered to you on a plate while you spend your days on the couch engrossed in Netflix.

- **Start with a breath and a bang**
Another reminder that up to eight minutes of mindful breathing or prayer nourishes your neural pathways and reinforces coherence in the heart, setting you up for success with clarity. Back this up with a list of the three most important things to do today that will have the largest impact and then

> Write down three things you are grateful for each morning and three things each night. Include the best aspects of yourself that you already feature instead of getting too stuck in what you're not.

take action on them. The latter is the most important part because goals are just dreams unless the tread hits the road at some stage.

- **See an Overwhelmologist**
Who's that? Mentors that tell you how they did it. They can break down where you want to be into bite-size pieces to help you get there. It could be someone working in your dream industry, another parent at school you admire, a successful uncle or a counsellor… a la moi!

- **Watch a thought leader online each week**
For those who don't like reading, you've got access to inspiration from reputable gurus on YouTube on your smartphone any day of the week on any topic, including relationships, real estate and finance to name a few. You can also tune into

any number of platforms now that offer audiobooks, so you can listen to them in the car or while out for your daily walk (see point number six…)

- **Self-compassion**

  I'm thinking golf days, horse riding weekends, day spas, silent retreats, flotation tanks, brewery tours, a bubbly bath at home or a book under a tree. Like me, I'm sure your to-do list is endless and it's important to *not* do as well. I even block gap time out on the calendar. Sometimes it's the only way you will know for sure that you will get that much-needed time out. Once you've locked it in—keep it there! All too often, me-time is the first thing to go when the calendar gets full.

- **Be grateful**

  Write down three things each morning and three things each night. Include the best aspects of yourself that you already feature instead of getting too stuck in what you're not. Stick them in a jar and enjoy reading your time capsule on days when you struggle to find one thing. This is a quick and easy way to pick yourself up and dust yourself off!

- **Build a 'feel good' tribe**

  Surround yourself with inspirational people. Unfriend those who consistently leave you feeling like a lesser version of yourself or who take on the form of 'energy vampires'. You know who they are because every time you finish hanging out with them, you just feel exhausted.

- **Experiment and learn a new thing each week**

  Fear will sure keep the lid on your wildly wonderful and potentially successful ideas. Think like a scientist who relentlessly experiments, searches, tests and tracks their progress. When in doubt, bias toward experiment and action!

The Effects of Stress

Stress has become a given in our daily lives and is quite often the first culprit in a long list of excuses about why we're unhappy. Stress comes from every single angle of our lives, from going to work, to running a household and trying to keep up with what kind of lifestyle social media says

> How you think about stress impacts your lifespan! But did you know that if you viewed 'controlled stress' as a really good thing, you'd be much better off within your relationship and life in general?

we should have. There has been some interesting research done on how our perception of the way stress affects our health can adversely increase your health and mortality.[15] How you think about stress impacts your lifespan! But did you know that if you viewed 'controlled stress' as a really good thing, you'd be much better off within your relationship and life in general?

Dr Caroline Leaf states that a healthy stress response, 'dilates the blood vessels around your heart, pumping blood and oxygen into your brain and releasing neurotransmitters, which work together to help you focus and think with clarity to react in the best way.' If it wasn't for stress, you wouldn't have made it to work, to university or wherever you needed to be this week. That's a healthy dose of stage one stress—when it facilitates you being alert and focused on the task at hand. Good stress gets you to an appointment on time or to the shops for milk because you know you'll be out tomorrow.

Stage two, however, is a prolonged version of the stage one stress response, with consistently increased cortisol in the bloodstream causing damage to our brains and bodies. As you could imagine, life for you and your partner will transform—and not in a good way— if there is a consistent stress response in your body. You will begin to subconsciously turn more of the good times into bad times. Stay even longer in this stress response state and you're in stage three. This is where your body is exhausted, leading to anxiety, depression, disease and worse.

Ultimately, stress comes from your thoughts. When you bottle them up and do not set them free in a healthy manner, they spill over, affecting your relationship. I see this often in couples that I work with, and I am conscious of it in my own relationship. Dr Leaf talks about the different levels of stress we mentioned above, in that many people have third-stage stress producing toxic cortisol levels within the body all the time.[16] Managing the sporting and social lives of three boys, a busy counselling practice and a full calendar of volunteering, community speaking and writing commitments all contribute to the worry that I might be at that stage three level sometimes. The important word there is 'sometimes'. I am constantly on the lookout for those physical signs of stress because I know the mental and emotional fallout won't be too far behind and *that* is when the damage is done to our relationships.

As Dr Leaf says, if you are always running on high stress you become stuck in a vice-like grip where you are holding onto resentment and unforgiveness.[17] Quite often, people present to my practice in this third stage state, not because they would normally consult a counsellor or psychologist or seek help from a mental health professional, but because they have reached the point where their relationship is in complete turmoil as a result of the way they are managing (or not managing) their stress.

The first step in presenting the best version of yourself is to be able to identify what your physical indicators of stress are. Is it:

- tightening throat sensation?
- aching jaw?
- sore neck?
- aching back?
- headaches?
- quick tempered?
- nail-biting?
- excessive sweating?
- grinding your teeth at night?
- sleeplessness?
- constantly worrying?

Maybe you are just mighty crabby most of the time?

These are just a few ways your body is yelling at you to try and get you to take notice of what's going on. It's important to pay attention to the physical signs in your body, especially when it comes to stress, as they are often indicators of what is happening for you mentally as well.

> Our intimate relationships should be a safe haven to express our raw feelings, to download and debrief.

When your body is shouting at you and you carry on oblivious, you may in turn be shouting at your partner for various things, ones that normally wouldn't trigger you into an emotional meltdown. Maybe your partner is yelling at you? Many couples have never even considered how often they are bringing their best, less stressed version of themselves to their marriage or relationship. Our intimate relationships should be a safe haven to express our raw feelings, to download and debrief. You are, however, ultimately responsible for maintaining your wellbeing and being an enjoyable, calm partner to be around in the long term.

Becoming aware of your stress levels and managing them is important not just for maintaining an effective and loving relationship, but for the health of your mind and body. Use the following ideas to help you manage the best, least stressed version of yourself:

Recognise and eliminate recurring distressing thoughts. Most of your conscious life, you are engaging in self-talk. How is that internal voice speaking to you? What sort of *I'm not... I can't...* language are you allowing yourself to think?

Find your element. Are you working in a job you love that uses all your talents? If the answer is no, now is the time to start a little investigative work. By finding your passion, work will no longer be a stressor in your world, but an enjoyable and satisfying event on your calendar for which you're rewarded. If your current commitments don't facilitate an imminent change, at least enjoy the process of revealing your strengths.

Get that check-up. Visit your preferred health professional for an overall wellbeing check, including an assessment of your diet and exercise. That's one less thing to stress over. Check any nagging ailments and be reassured that they are accounted for and aren't leading to something more serious.

Journal moments of severe anxiety. Ask yourself, *what triggered that anxiety?* Address it and importantly, seek help to change your approach.

Laugh...find your inner jester. Try coughing first then see if you can turn it into a laughing sound. Furthermore, by adjusting your posture from stooped to upright, your mind can very well believe you are calmer.

Stretch! (and make it a loooooooooooong stretch). If exercise doesn't fit your agenda—stretching in the comfort and privacy of your home can prepare you for that badly needed aerobic exercise that releases natural chemicals to combat stress.

Visualisation. Use your powerful imagination! It is difficult to will yourself into a calm state, but you can certainly imagine it. Your mind will follow.

Confide in a good listener. It helps to talk with your partner, loved ones or a counsellor. Sometimes an expert outside your circle can relieve your internal pressure cooker so it won't explode and have a detrimental impact on your relationship.

The power of silence, meditation or prayer. Even just a few minutes a day can make a difference! When we meditate, our mind naturally begins to relax and 'sink' into deeper levels of rest. I'll 'sink' deeper into explaining why.

In the white matter of the brain, there is a fatty substance called *myelin*. It is a 'sheath' that protects nerve fibres, inhibits energy loss and helps information move along neural pathways. When you repeat an activity, the myelin coating thickens in those areas used and information travels faster along the neural highways associated with that task.

In the same way, meditation, prayer and mindfulness activities that involve attending to the sensations in the here and now, energise certain layers of the neocortex in your brain and add thickness to the prefrontal cortex and insula. When you pay attention to your breathing, heart rate, muscles, feelings or desires, the left hemisphere of your pre-frontal cortex turns on and prevents your right hemisphere from obscuring your thoughts with negativity. This encourages you to approach life with greater clarity and fervour versus becoming easily overwhelmed and anxious when faced with challenging tasks.

The Force of Forgiveness

Do you ever wonder why people who experience incredible adversity come out the other end joyful and kind? It seems one key difference in these individuals is their inclination to forgive. Whether they choose to forgive themselves or their perpetrators has a great deal to do with what follows in their lives. Those that choose anger and hold their grudges seem bitter and tortured their whole lives. The decision not to forgive can be toxic—both to yourself and to your relationship.

By the time couples are finally sitting in front of me in my practice, they are sick of fighting. They've been on the 'he-said-she-said' and the 'you-did-this, no-I-didn't' rides for a long time and now they desperately want to get off. It is a lonely ride and they have generally been trapped in pain and isolation for long periods.

> Forgiveness is a choice, an act of your free will.

Sound familiar? If it does, it might be time to work on your ability to forgive.

Forgiveness is a choice, an act of your free will. I am fascinated by the numerous studies that have shown that when we don't forgive and then later revisit our memories of the supposed wrongdoing, a fear response is produced in our amygdala (the part of our brain responsible for our emotions).[18] This response causes a release of stress hormones, which increases our heart rate and blood pressure. If we keep holding on to our betrayals and anger, the fear response remains active, putting us at risk of developing stress-related illness both mentally and physically.[19] Refusing to forgive allows the perceived wrongdoer the ability to live rent-free in our head for far too long, while we lie awake at night ruminating.

David listened intently during a session when his wife of twenty-five years, Samantha, began to recount a story from long ago. She appeared embarrassed and pained as she softy detailed an event from their time together. She told a story from her wedding day to David—but it was not a story of joy. I listened as she relived the pain she felt when three of her pretty and thinner bridesmaids laughed and joked whilst all perched on David's lap. Despite revealing her embarrassment, the following day, he'd discounted her feelings as 'silly' and 'jealous'. She's still thinking about it a quarter of a century later! Now, that moment had grown beyond its original significance because she had continued adding grievances to it throughout their marriage. Twenty-five years later, she was still incredibly upset about it. Imagine the toxic weight she could have jettisoned from their relationship if, when she had bravely communicated her embarrassment and pain at the outset of the incident, he had provided a receptive listening ear and empathy. He certainly downplayed the whole scenario in our session and would never have fraternised innocently if he'd known the long-term ramifications. I've rarely seen a malicious, nasty spouse in my counselling room; however, I've also rarely seen a spouse demonstrate sincere empathy on a topic they disagree on—that is, until I've finished with them! (Note: Malicious, violent domestic cases are referred for specialised support and refuge and are not applicable to this discussion.)

One thing for sure is that again and again, I notice couples trapped in the vice of unforgiveness for many years longer than is necessary.

Having said that, forgiving others is not easy. I assure you; many clients have attempted to hurl my 'How to Forgive' worksheet back in my face over the years. Just like any other new or difficult task, you need to learn how to do it with repetition and consistency. I passionately believe forgiveness is necessary for the sake of your emotional wellbeing, as well as that of your partner. Here's the link for the worksheet at www.relationshiprejuvenator.com/forgive.

If you struggle to forgive, these five tips may help:

Slow it down. Ensure you are not in a heightened emotional state. Allow 20 minutes for your heart rate to slow down, then ask yourself these questions to gain a clearer perspective: *How is s/he feeling right now? Are they justified in their actions? What is my part in this?* Putting yourself in someone else's shoes is no easy task—especially when it comes to your spouse.

Switch off the nasty voice. We all have an inner voice, and sometimes it doesn't play nicely. When we fight, its critical nature comes to the fore, spewing forth things like, *he's trying to manipulate you,* or, *she's twisting your words again,* or, *just ignore him, you'll feel better that way.* All of this is counter-productive

> Every day, shift your focus from what you don't like to what you do like! What you focus on attracts more of the same. Express gratitude three times a day to your partner.

to forgiveness. In the heat of emotion, replacing these statements with kind and respectful self-talk such as *'This is his best attempt at coping.'* or *'This is temporary and we can resolve this.'* is paramount to moving forward and playing fairly.

It's a choice. Rather than holding on to all the little things your partner has done (I know you know what I mean—we all have a vast catalogue of wrongdoings stored in our brain!) you must begin that choice to leave it behind you. You will have conflict;

that is human nature. But choose not to hold onto the upsets. Work through the current issue by listening and validating and grow together from it.

Ditch the baggage. Whether you like it or not, your childhood and parent/carer relationship role models play a big part in the relationship you have with your partner. Perhaps you had a parent who used silence to let you know they were angry. Consequently, each time your partner is quiet, you find yourself wondering, *what have I done?* Your partner, on the other hand, may just be tired and having a quiet moment. Work out where your fear stems from, put it into context and evaluate your behaviour from this logical, rational standpoint.

Who will win? When you're in the thick of an argument, it's very hard to 'see the forest for the trees'. You lose track of the goal of being on the same side (a tenet of any good partnership) because you're so concerned with winning. But for you to win, your partner needs to lose. Is this the outcome you truly want?

Every day, shift your focus from what you don't like to what you do like! What you focus on attracts more of the same. Express gratitude three times a day to your partner. Anything counts, from the ordinary to the extraordinary. You'll marvel at how this new positivity and acknowledgment shifts the energy of your relationship.

Set yourself the goal of cooperation and make a commitment to flexing your forgiveness muscle and start to watch your relationship pump with synergy.

TAKEAWAY TOOLS

You cannot ask your significant other to make 'you' better, nor can you lay the breakdown of your relationship solely at their feet. Taking responsibility for your contribution to your relationship is one of the most powerful things you can do to begin the healing process with your partner. In time, working on the best version of you will ensure you immediately feel better about yourself and those around you, and in particular, your spouse or partner.

- Give up the blame game. There are always at least two people in a relationship contributing to the way it is suffering or flourishing.
- Present the best version of yourself in your relationship. Self-reflect on whether you are truly being the best you can be for your partner.
- Nurture yourself. Get healthy socially, physically and mentally, using the SEEDS acronym.
- Recognise and eliminate recurring distressing thoughts. Stress is a factor that affects everyone in all aspects of their lives, but only you can choose how to deal with the three stages of stress appropriately.
- Your healthy perspective on stress is incredibly important to realising that it is not all bad.

- Practice the five tips of forgiveness. It is the key to moving toward joy in your relationship so forgiveness should be your daily intention.

Renovate Your Relationship

RELATIONSHIP STATUS?

Consider your relationship as a wonderful 'self-improvement' project. When you are not afraid to hold up a mirror and pay attention to your actions, you will see the kind of energy you provide to your spouse's environment.

The health of any relationship is difficult to determine from a perspective of aloof detachment. Think of it like a doctor trying to diagnose a patient from across the room with limited information and no communication. The patient complains of stomach pain, so the doctor knows there is a problem, but is it gas that could be relieved with a gentle walk or a ruptured appendix requiring major surgery? Taking a scalpel to a minor problem is unnecessary and likely to cause further damage.

Partners who fail to take ownership for their contribution to closed or harsh communication will inhibit diagnosing what is failing. Consider your relationship as a wonderful 'self-improvement' project. When you are not afraid to hold up a mirror and pay attention to your actions, you will see the kind of energy you provide to your spouse's environment. This brave openness to feedback won't tickle, but neither does removing an inflamed appendix!

There are several recurrent pain points for couples, which require both partners to address.

Naked to the Soul

Here are a couple more analogies. You are out and insanely hungry. You try to ignore the growling in your stomach, all the while hoping somebody else notices and offers you a snack. Maybe you'll just wait to see if it subsides before you pass out.

No?

How about when you're a guest at a new friend's house and are feeling ridiculously thirsty; should you simply hope to forget about it before your mouth turns into a 'cocky's' cage and you can't speak?

> Turn the pages of your life, and you'll notice that your highlight reel features sharing great moments with others, and feeling loved, valued or appreciated.

Still no?

The reason is somewhat obvious. Not communicating that you're hungry or thirsty is a bad idea: you can literally die if you hide those sorts of needs for too long! Even if you're one of those people who doesn't like to bother others, chances are the discomfort you feel when your hunger or thirst becomes serious enough will override your politeness and you'll do something to help yourself. Let's apply this kind of thinking to a relationship. Grab a drink or something to eat and stay with me on this one.

Everyone has a history, and sometimes they're not the shiniest of backgrounds. Sequential life setbacks can leave emotional scars. I can guarantee everyone on this planet has suffered rejection and all the devastating effects of being alienated, disappointed and lonely. When this is repeatedly experienced as a child and that child makes the decision to avoid relying on others at all costs, the resulting loneliness can be particularly long-lasting. Translate this behaviour to the intimate relationship of an adult and even an adult can find it challenging to reach out and enjoy closeness. It can make us cynical, pessimistic and give up entirely on the idea of ever finding love. Every new failure can become a brick in the wall between you and other people. Once that wall is up, one of two things happen; either you refuse to let other people through that wall, or you refuse to let yourself *out* from behind it.

Now you're withholding love.

You've already read my frequently used theme, 'we are designed relationally'. That is, we feel safe and secure when we know we can turn to our loved ones for support, love and connection. Turn the pages of your life, and you'll notice that your highlight reel features sharing great moments with others, and feeling loved, valued or appreciated.

Where do we start?

We get 'naked to the soul', a term gifted to me by one of my wise counselling supervisors, Peter Janetzki. This is about getting authentic with your own needs and turning on what emotionally focussed therapists term your 'attachment antennae' to a healthy frequency. Those who've enjoyed positive childhood experiences of connecting with their parents or caregivers naturally tend to extend this to their romantic relationships. Those who've experienced a less than ideal childhood can feel a sense of loss and emptiness for what was missed.

As a result, our inherent need to survive and feel safe prompts some people to turn up their antennae or alert button to perceived rejection from others. They can be hypersensitive and experience symptoms of anxiety when they sense others might let them down. They can be clingy and needy or try to control their partner to keep safe. Alternatively, those who keep their antennae turned down too low in an effort to ensure they stay independent, tend to avoid closeness and keep their distance. The use of either frequency is their best attempt to cope with or avoid the insecurity from a threatened bond with those closest and dear to them.

> Is it possible that we don't even recognise our desire for love? Perhaps it is hidden by our underlying need for belonging and acceptance for being ourselves with all our flaws and raw spots.

Often people will try to protect themselves from getting hurt by depriving themselves of love. This, unfortunately, is not the best nutrition plan for a healthy relationship. The lack of communication creates assumptions, drama, confusion and a feeling of insecurity. Your newfound love will eventually wither through lack of emotional food and water because that wall is up, keeping back the one thing a relationship needs to thrive—intimacy. It's like purposely leaving out the eggs in your cake recipe—the very thing that binds all the ingredients together.

Understanding the root cause behind anxious or avoidant behaviours is integral to appreciating and respecting you or your partner's need for space or responsiveness.

Toolbox Topic Three: Relationship Status?

It would be safe to say that our human nature's default status is to lack appreciation for ourselves. Even worse, some people's default tends towards self-deprecation and toxic self-loathing. It takes considerable effort to keep abreast of the anxious spiralling thoughts that feed this state. In society, when you talk yourself up or display too much self-promotion—you're arrogant, conceited and 'full of yourself'. In reality, we thrive on encouragement, positive reinforcement and the connectedness from others to 'have our back', particularly when life gets challenging.

If I were to blatantly stereotype, many men will derive status from their achievements along with power from sex. A lot of women feel validated for their appearance and enjoy a sense of belonging and acceptance when in a relationship. I note that we do have unique 'mosaic' brains so everyone features their unique blend of longings.

When we 'strip back' our work, our interests, our looks and who we are with, it's worth reflecting on exactly, 'Who am I without my money, job or whatever I rely on for validation?', 'Who do I represent?', 'What do I stand for?' and 'What do I long for?'.

Do we miss out on complementing each other in healthy partnerships because we overlook what is actually inhibiting intimacy? Is it possible that we don't even recognise our desire for love? Perhaps it is hidden by our underlying need for belonging and acceptance for being ourselves with all our flaws and raw spots. Are we scared of what we will see in ourselves when not covered by our 'things'?

You deserve to ask (in the appropriate way) for your deepest desires, to be recognised as an amazing work in progress and to be accepted for your short-comings. Have the courage to turn up bare in your relationship, naked to the soul.

Withholding love in/from a relationship is what withholding hunger or thirst is to living; it's not going to end well. So how do you know whether you are withholding love? It is not always as cut and dried as you might think, as a lot of the things we do and say come from a subconscious level. They are driven by behaviours we've learnt along the way as part of the legacy given to us from the people around us when we were growing up. Our partners on the receiving end (or rather, *not* receiving end) can probably identify the existence of these walls very easily, even if we mightn't be aware of them.

Look through these red flags and identify whether you might be withholding love:

- You reject feedback and your reflex is to blame your partner.
- Complimenting your spouse is uncomfortable.
- Despite knowing their Love Language[20]—whether your partner prefers to receive gifts, touch, acts of service, words of affirmation or quality time—you're unable to meet their needs. Read more on this in Toolbox Topic Five.
- Conflict means you are silent and emotionally unavailable.
- It's easier to criticise than to find positives in your partner.
- Activities such as work, volunteering, social media, internet, books and other friends take priority over quality relationship time.
- You avoid sex or do not actively participate.
- Porn has become an addiction as it doesn't require emotional attentiveness.
- Authentic feeling words are off the table.
- You exhibit controlling behaviours.

Toolbox Topic Three: Relationship Status?

If you can identify with or are displaying any of the 'hangry-like' (that's hungry/angry) symptoms above, here are some questions to ponder. They may help you figure out how you can shift your behaviours and start to let some of those intimacy walls crumble. Being truthful and honest with your answers will help you to see not just *what* you're withholding, but may give some insight into *why*.

Consider:

- What profound, beautiful and joyful thought have you not shared with your partner?
- Can you recall an experience that was so poignant, fantastic, or gratifying that you didn't know how to talk about it?
- When you feel a little aggravated and critical, what behaviours do you exhibit?
- Are you afraid of the response when you sincerely share and allow yourself to be vulnerable?
- Do you feel you have the right to assertively ask for what you need in your relationship?
- What self-talk may have started up as a result of soul-destroying words from any previous relationships?
- Have you found peace and freedom from forgiving either yourself or others for betrayal, disappointment and grief?

You'd be surprised what you can learn and achieve through some serious introspection. Validate your ingenious inherent design to adopt self-preservation behaviours to propel you towards pleasure and away from pain (resulting from past hurts). Don't expect the walls to come down immediately, but hopefully now that you have something meaty in your tucker-bag, you'll realise how to recognise the signs that you are withholding love, and what you're missing out on. You'll have some prompts for self-reflection and will be able to adjust your responses as a result, which in turn will quench that emotional thirst and satiate your hunger for a joyful relationship.

Sex or Ice Cream?

If I asked you 'What is one of the most thrilling, magical and unforgettable experiences in your life? Would it be that last tub of cookie dough ice cream you ate? Or would it be meeting your true love, committing your lives to each other and becoming sexually intimate?'

Which experience is the basis of your emotional well-being? Gives a sense of security? Or provides your own personal mirror of self-development? Hint: you won't find it at the bottom of your freezer.

> The early days of your relationship are high in helpful oxytocin, the feel-good hormone. Oxytocin helps us pair up! We take more risks, are out to impress and less likely to consider consequences.

Intimacy changes and empowers us. Starry-eyed, we each leverage the other's point of view and skills as we navigate life together. Access to shared resources can increase our belief in our ability to reach our goals, personally and as a team. As 'you and me' become 'we', the initial rush of increased intimacy is a heady and exciting experience. However, for many couples, as time goes on this becomes anything but.

As a marriage therapist, I have the sacred honour of listening to the moving accounts from both men and women as they experience baring it all to each other, even their souls. From where I sit, the incredibly private admissions of each partner are from places which can be so secret, can mean so much and can create a complex myriad of good and bad consequences. In the therapy room, we sometimes marvel about the sexual differences between the quick-light gas-oven type blokes versus the electric slow burn female version. We muse over the way one partner will think nothing of giving the 'tap on the shoulder' after a day of tense and silent conflict, whilst the other retreats in shock, preferring a more communicative approach to re-connect first. Then there is the heartache of those who struggle with not fulfilling the sex-crazed stereotype, whilst their partner correspondingly grapples with feeling sexually unattractive and ugly. Sex: it means so much.

The early days of your relationship are high in helpful oxytocin, the feel-good hormone. Oxytocin helps us pair up! We take more risks, are out to impress and less likely to consider consequences. With the help of sexual intimacy, amazing, almost mysterious bonds between partners are created. It's an incredible union of souls that brings couples together. But as time goes on, for a large range of reasons, we don't always put in as much effort with physical intimacy, taking the other person for granted or ignoring their requests more and more frequently. As a result, your spouse is less likely to feel amorous, resulting in fewer opportunities for the sense of value and connection derived from hanky-panky.

Many people connect a real sense of feeling valued to sex, rather than viewing it just as an arbitrary opportunity to 'get their rocks off!' Stereotypically, the role of the highly sexed partner was assigned to men, while women have been portrayed as the distinct opposite, but this is not always the case.

Many couples compare their frequency of intercourse with others, but it is mutual satisfaction and not the frequency that matters. In my counselling practice, if a couple is enjoying sex just on their birthdays, then I'm happy if they're happy! The challenge arises when one partner wants it every other day and the other is only interested in having sex once a month. For those with a higher sex drive than their partner, not

> There are a significant proportion of libidinous females out there who suffer inextricably from rejection and low self-esteem as a result of not being with a man who fits the stereotypical oversexed male.

having sex can be a big problem, with some people getting to the point of barely being able to function without it. Maybe those partners need to step up and make an effort just because it is important. *Whoa!* Controversial, I know.

Equally, perhaps, we all need to work at being alluring, too. If you smell, don't look after yourself and are steadily working on your beer gut or muffin top, then your partner probably isn't going to be dancing in the sheets with you in a hurry. Each spouse needs to ask what they are doing to make sex an attractive prospect for the other. It may well even start with emptying the dishwasher!

It is never too late to begin to have the courage to address any such canoodling conundrums and speak to a professional therapist. In the meantime, here are some things to consider and think about concerning your sex life:

Toolbox Topic Three: Relationship Status?

- Are we able to comfortably talk about this topic together? For some, stepping up might mean just mustering up the courage to talk to each other about intimacy issues.
- Did I go into this relationship with an unrealistic expectation of having the same libido as my spouse all the time?
- Do we regularly set aside a sacred space in our lives for sex and give it the attention it deserves?
- Do we try to save some of the best of ourselves for each other? How are your energy and fitness levels? Are you getting sufficient sleep, exercise and eating a healthy diet?
- Do I pay attention to my appearance to ensure I feel confident, handsome or sexy?
- In what ways can I healthily learn to find joy in sex for my long-term mental health and the longevity of my marriage, especially where my ability to do so may have been damaged by previous experiences?
- What are the consequences of my decisions on my family and community, potentially for many generations to come, if I'm thinking of seeking sex elsewhere?

Within my counselling rooms, men frequently ask me why women don't desire sexual intimacy as much as men. Again, I highlight that it's just not appropriate to stereotype men and women. There are a significant proportion of libidinous females out there who suffer inextricably from rejection and low self-esteem as a result of not being with a man who fits the stereotypical oversexed male. Sex therapist Laurie Watson of Psychology Today[21] provides this insight:

- A man's body chemistry—especially with that well-known hormone testosterone surging through his body—has a lot to do with generally having a higher desire for sex.
- A woman's passion is more likely ignited in her mind by contented feelings of connection, adoration and positive memories.
- Men crave sex like chocolate—it's a hunger to be fulfilled.
- The energy derived from sexual pleasure can be a tantalising reward for working, monotony and protecting his family.
- Turning on his partner is reported to be the most satisfying element of their pursuit to make it a mutually pleasurable experience. According to Watson, many men fantasise about improving on the sexual satisfaction of their partner.

For men, sex is not just about 'getting his rocks off,' but a deep emotional connection that creates attachment. As Watson aptly states, when a man feels desired by his partner, this 'spurs relational generosity, faith and optimism'. It strengthens a sense of reassurance and commitment. Women, on the other hand, generally long for an emotional connection before physical connection and it's worth realising that they may need that first in order to be emotionally vulnerable and available to communicate about sex.

The differences between how partners approach sex cannot be assigned to their gender, but the most important thing to remember is that physical intimacy represents a large part of your relationship, no matter how frequently or infrequently you're doing it.

Lost Yourself in Your Relationship?

Great relationships feature a healthy sense of self, independence and interdependence. Interdependence means being mutually dependent. You have flexibility and reciprocity without controlling behaviours.

It can be a delicate balance that may have you relying on or conforming to your partner too much, leaving you without purpose or direction. Alternatively, too much independence can leave you living like flatmates with little support from each another and no chance of attaining joint goals. When there is mutual recognition and respect for personal space and individuality, your intimate relationship flourishes.

> When there is mutual recognition and respect for personal space and individuality, your intimate relationship flourishes.

When you've achieved that wonderful balance, your relationship features:

- Friendship
- Ongoing affirmation, encouragement and adoration
- Sexual intimacy and mutual gratification
- Respect for differing values
- Time together and time apart
- Mutually enjoyable activities as well as different interests
- The ability to actively help others, but not to the exclusion of your partnership
- Support when your 'chips are down'
- Trust

With many years of counselling under my belt, I notice common themes in couples when things start to go askew. Often, it is very much related to that delicate balance between independence and interdependence.

For example, one or both partners may suffer from a low sense of worth, experiencing a 'primal panic' of neediness when the other seeks time alone or with other friends. There could be an absence of trust, stemming from experiences from either the current or previous relationships, which undermines the ability to allow or enjoy freedom.

> Know that you're not designed or predetermined to be the shadow of your spouse, nor their dictator! You were created with the freedom and responsibility to complement them.

There could be unequal power structures where one partner is too dominant, or an environment where important values such as religion, family culture or parenting styles are not supported or encouraged, causing distress.

Major life events, such as starting a family, can result in mothers losing their alone time, financial freedom and involvement in major family decisions.

Sometimes this balance becomes out of whack over time without either partner realising it. The addition of children, financial changes or health issues can distract couples from their relationship and begin to skew a relationship slightly off course. The longer it is off course, the larger the problems become before they are noticed. So how do we achieve the golden balance of independence and interdependence? Some questions for couples to ask are:

Toolbox Topic Three: Relationship Status?

- Do you have an adequate sense of self-worth that supports healthy boundaries and enables you to assertively seek time out and also ask for quality time together?
- Do you lack boundaries that allow your partner to be too dominant?
- If you are told you're too controlling, consider this: what needs are you seeking to meet by governing your spouse's life? Know where you end and where your partner begins and start behaving accordingly. Do you need to relinquish some control? Perhaps stop doing things for your partner that s/he can easily do themselves?
- Can you rebuild broken trust in this relationship, or do you need to heal from the scars of hurt from the past?

Know that you're not designed or predetermined to be the shadow of your spouse, nor their dictator! You were created with the freedom and responsibility to complement them. When you enjoy this wonderful balance, you're free to express your thoughts, feelings and desires. You can stand firm when your principles and values are compromised. You also openly welcome the opinions of your partner and remain considerate of alternative perspectives besides your own. Regularly find this synergy and you will both shine as even better versions of yourselves, grounded in mutual admiration, encouragement and respect.

Getting the Balance Right

By the time couples seek out someone like me to help them unravel the knots that have gradually formed in their relationship, there are more often than not some major issues to deal with. There are so many wonderful strategies all couples could be using to ensure that intimacy of the emotional, spiritual and physical kind is ever-present between them. This is just as much about renovating and renewing your mind as your relationship.

Here are some tips:

Indulge in you first! Make a list of 30 things that delight you. Carve out time to do three things in the next week and be responsible for achieving them. Focus on your desires. It is not your partner's job to make you happy. Forget why you can't or why it won't work. You absolutely CAN stack small habits that are anchored in your daily rituals that make your list possible. For example, 'After I've had breakfast each morning, I will set the timer and spend eight minutes outside on the deck, enjoying the fresh air and practising deep breathing and prayer.' Repetition and consistency are paramount to your new-found self-compassion to avoid losing yourself along the way.

Chat. Call a trusted friend who can also support you. Feedback from the counselling room is that women generally have too many words for a bloke to bear, so share them around with other members of the fairer sex. For the men, think about going fishing or catching up with a mate for a cold one to get social and open the door to communication if something is on your mind. Particularly here in Australia, it's my opinion that the stereotypes of gender socialisation prevent you from openly communicating your inner world.

What is your relationship newsreel? If I were to ask you what are the first three words that come to mind when asked to describe your partner, would that indicate a healthy and realistic approach to your relationship?

TAKEAWAY TOOLS

Relationships suffer from many conscious and subconscious issues, which can impact negatively on both partners regardless of who brings the 'issue' to the table. Identifying some of the common pain points and working to overcome them will bring more joy and less friction to your relationship.

- Don't withhold love. Communication is a key component within loving relationships; break down those walls and invest in the power of words with your partner.
- Intimacy of the emotional and sexual kind is influenced by so many things, from our gender, to our hormones and past experiences. Again, open communication and support is the key to a joyful relationship.
- It is crucial to get the balance of independence and interdependence within any relationship just right so that we are complementing, rather than completing, each other.
- Relationships are meant to be wonderful, joyful and supportive places to be. Within our busy lives, each partner must make an effort to nurture the relationship with the love and attention it deserves. Don't give up! Find your passion for each other.

CONFLICT

There isn't one kind of man or one kind of woman. No one will ever completely conform to a stereotype; you just won't fit. You are unique.

You've fallen hook, line and sinker if you've bought into the belief you can cruise through a relationship without a disagreement. Conflict is caused by personality differences and values that differ. They're inevitable and normal! Strangely enough, though, it's not uncommon for couples I work with to openly admit they avoid conflict at all costs. Unfortunately, this method of problem-solving can lead to relationships becoming increasingly icy below the surface as resentment sets in and the iceberg grows too large for the Love Boat to navigate around.

The Gender Blender

Before we get into the often-bemoaned differences between genders, let's point out the amazing similarity between them—we all long to be loved! Yes, we might look different, sound different and go about getting love differently, but all the PhD'ers out there keep coming back to more similarities than differences. For example, one comparison study of 1400 brains using magnetic resonance imaging found that up to half of them contained common features in both male and female brains.[22]

The highly regarded neuroscientist Dr Sarah McKay spoke to journalist Lynne Malcolm from ABC's Radio National program, *All In The Mind*. I'm sure you'd agree with Dr McKay's observation during the interview—'There seems to be an assumption that all women have a female brain and all men have a male brain and we can sort ourselves into a pink bucket and a blue bucket by virtue of our brain structure and our brain function.'[23] She says there is indigo, violet and in between! What *does* influence our unique brain structures are life experiences, expectations, feelings and mindset.

I had the pleasure of meeting Dr McKay at an 'International Association of Applied Neuroscience' conference and she subsequently highlighted during our Salt106.5 radio interview, that male and female brains are a lot more similar than different. You just can't separate them into two groups of male and female people based on the anatomy of their genitals. Instead, we should consider our amazing brains as 'unique mosaics of different features, some male-like, some female-like, with plenty of features best described as androgynous.'[24] We feature a beautiful, unique blend.

Whilst there are variances in our brain structures, one important point is that we are miraculously designed to complement each other. When you think about it, there isn't one kind of man or one kind of woman. No one will ever completely conform to a stereotype; you just won't fit. You are unique. Having said that, there are some common traits we can assign to each sex, most of which are supported by science.

Whilst the late American journalist Helen Rowland certainly didn't have a degree in science, she astutely sums up how communication amongst couples can change over time;

'Before marriage, a man declares that he would lay down his life to serve you; after marriage, he won't even lay down his newspaper to talk to you.'[25]

The conundrum of communication between couples, where one barely says two words and the other can't shut up, is another major theme within the counselling room, especially when it comes to resolving conflict and maintaining a respectful, loving relationship.

The fact is, constructive emotional disclosure discussions support closeness. I get the impression that aside from the closeness part, this seems most unappealing to men. One helpful male wrote to me in response to a men's series I penned for the Sunshine Coast Daily's relationships column with this insightful perspective; 'The masculine in all of us, men and women, is covert by nature and thus reluctant to open itself up to scrutiny. Many men, especially those who have yet to recognise the power of their own feminine essence, simply have not exercised this channel for connection with another human being.' Quite simply, men don't usually get gabby because they're not predominantly hardwired that way. Which is not to say they can't connect new wires!

In this excerpt from Dr Caroline Leaf's book *Who Switched Off Your Brain? Solving the Mystery of He Said, She Said*[26] the difference is clear:

'A husband may find it a challenge to keep up with his wife as she zig-zags her way through all the various adventures of her day, constantly inserting random factoids and minutiae. There's a reason she knows where she's going, even when he's completely lost and beginning to lose interest. Her girlfriends love all the extra details she gives when she's telling a story—her husband's wondering, 'what does this have to do with that?'

The difference in what is considered important within the above communication can be found in the emotional centre of our brains. Female brains have an amazing capacity to group sounds and analyse them. By contrast, the male brain listens for a specific focussed purpose.

> Female brains have an amazing capacity to group sounds and analyse them. By contrast, the male brain listens for a specific focussed purpose.

Women have a stronger left amygdala that facilitates recall of emotional experiences in more detail. One male client made me laugh out loud with his joke, 'Never lie to women with big foreheads. They never forget easily as they're hiding at least one terabyte in there.' He's right, except that even without a larger forehead, women will remember all those times when they've been hurt, disappointed and shocked by your behaviour in more detail than you blokes would understandably prefer. Men are stronger on the right side, providing them with the ability to focus on the big picture in a more practical and orderly way. Guys are also fortunate to have a slightly smaller prefrontal cortex, which allows them to get to the point a lot quicker, with reason and logic.

A woman's amygdala is more easily activated by emotions compared to their man's action-orientated and practical response, which is more alert to danger and wired for protecting. You threaten them, and then they'll exhibit more emotion! This practical, external focus explains why he always wants to fix it without the need for long talks into the night just as his female partner revs up to go in verbal circles for hours with no apparent point. Simply put, his brain circuits aren't wired to retain information in the detailed and emotional way of a woman. How on earth are we then expected to communicate in the same way as our partner?

As I regularly highlight in couples therapy, ladies—save some of your words for your gal pals and reduce any extravagant body movements to minimise distraction! Fellas, hang in there with us. Keep eye-contact, reassure, ask questions and practise attentive listening for as long as you can. Stop pondering the footy scores or other bouncy things—we see it all over your face! As Dr Leaf covers in *Who Switched Off Your Brain?*, neuroscience reveals females are extremely accomplished at detecting whether they're being listened to—or not.[27] It influences our sense of self-worth and we will catch you out!

Another communication question men ask is, 'Why do women always interpret the worst of what men are trying to say and not just assume the best case?'

'Trying to say' are the important words here. I can't count the number of times brave blokes have turned up for counselling rather ill-equipped to reveal what's really going on for them and even worse, attempt to talk about the 'f' word—feelings. For both men and women, if you've rarely spoken about how you feel emotionally, perhaps never, this can be a major roadblock along the path to relationship joy. I do wonder how much socialisation has created this stoicism and repression of feelings that contribute to men (and some women) leaving the 'relationship stuff' up to their partner.

Males are not the 'feelingless' gender—they're in there! If many Australian blokes haven't traditionally been encouraged to speak about matters of the heart and this is then coupled with a brain that tends to internalise, why would they naturally and expressively reveal their emotions to openly communicate the way women want and create that connection we all long for in our relationships? For many, it's as unnatural as breathing underwater.

This lack of experience and unwillingness to speak about their feelings may also have been com-

> Could we shift the blame to a more collaborative approach to enjoy our fascinating and different approaches to communicating?

pounded unwittingly by their chattier partner. It's worth noting that sometimes, based on previous experience, some women have already labelled their man with certain unfavourable traits, jumping to the 'worst-case scenario' on everything from fidelity to finances. Do we also incorporate 'catastrophic' thinking into our relationships, that then translates to a lack of trust and looking for the negative in all situations? Do we attempt to mindread in making weird and wonderful assumptions, instead of giving them the benefit of the doubt? Does comparison steal the joy from hearing the positives in your man's communication as compared to what you hear other men say to their partner?

Maybe you assume all other men say all the right things and forget the positive traits and words your partner does get right in a different way? I whole-heartedly agree that many men could share the 'relationship load' in facilitating emotional attentiveness, however, could those same ladies remove any high expectations and the 'shoulds'? Could we shift the blame to a more collaborative approach to enjoy your fascinating and different approaches to communicating? Why not play the 'Catch Them Doing It Well' game for a change?

Beyond a doubt, the differences in the way men and women communicate are clear, but that doesn't mean that communication should cease altogether. When that happens, lots of other wonderful parts of the relationship like trust, intimacy and support also cease, with conflict being the only thing bound to flourish.

How about when she sees 'puce' and he sees brown? She sees 'steel slate' and he sees grey. Men and women *do* see through different lenses in many instances. Realising this masculine versus feminine approach could be one major step forward to your more intimate relationship.

A perplexed Jason contacted me during a series I wrote in my newspaper column for men on understanding their perspective being in a relationship with a woman. He conveyed his frustration at constantly being questioned by his partner about interior decorating colour options. He noted, 'We only see in primary colours', and he's quite right! Men do see multiple distinct colours only and females see multiple shades. It's hard-wired.

As you could imagine, women become quite despondent and feel rejected when we receive little input to our dilemma of the 'mango tango' curtains versus the coral ones. Gratitude to Dr Leaf for the following excerpt from her book, *He Said She Said*, as she provides greater insight around the cause of this due to the biology involved in our vision![28]

'The X-chromosome provides the cone-shaped cells that handle colour. Women have two X-chromosomes and men have one, so women have more cells that allow them to see subtle changes in shades of colour. Females also have more P-cells—special cells in the retina that help the brain interpret texture and colour. These P-cells allow women to be more detail-oriented

> I love the use of the simplistic word 'Ouch' to convey when you're hurt. This will also diffuse your reactive torrent of words and still signals to your partner that they've hit a 'raw spot'.

than men. Males, on the other hand, have more M-cells, other specialised cells in the retina that help the brain analyse motion, action and direction. M-cells help men see how things move and work.'

Maybe this research about how men and women see colour differently makes it easier to see why there can be gaps in our communication.

This would explain why I've managed to reverse into my husband's car in our driveway—let's just say more than once—in broad daylight. It also makes sense why he couldn't care less about what shade of red he went when he found out. Surely the fact that men see better than women in bright light and women see more details in short distances in the dark has something to do with it?

Drowning in conflict? When supporting couples, I need to help them understand factors such as their key underlying emotions and triggers during conflict, however, here are some more simple points you can easily consider as a first step:

Realise what it is you're arguing about

It's not about right or wrong. It's about two people who have different thoughts and opinions. It doesn't mean you don't love the other person and usually, no one has malicious intent. You're a human being trying to get along with another human being and it is quite okay not to agree all of the time.

Work out how important it is to each of you

Realistically rank on a one to ten scale the question: 'How much does this mean to me?' For one of you, the glossy versus the matt paint for the bedroom might be very important. For your partner, it might be fairly irrelevant and more about criticism, financial values or seeking to be heard.

Find out why it's that important

If someone ranks their choice of walnut timber kitchen cupboards with a forest painted feature wall over the black and grey stainless-steel look as high number on the above scale, there's probably a reason. Listen to that reason. Show empathy to your partner as well as active listening. Avoid 'correcting' their reasoning. If this is important to you both, read on further and TRI Bonding.

Recognise you've been triggered

Own the reality that you might not know why it is so important—only that it is! Be present with yourself, take a deep breath and check in with your ego; is it simply that it might be hungry for a feed? I love the use of the simplistic word 'Ouch' to convey when you're hurt. This will also diffuse your reactive torrent of words and still signals to your partner that they've hit a 'raw spot'.

Keep it focussed

Don't bring other is-
sues or arguments
into your current con-
versation. That goes
for any disagreement,

> Bottling up your emotions is a fast
> track to an even worse problem, so
> it's important to get it out in the
> open and deal with the issue like
> adults.

ever. If you find that you **can't** address which kitchen cupboard
materials without mentioning what happened last week, guess
what? That's likely an issue you need to be addressing first.

Work as a team to find a solution

Sometimes there might need to be more of a respectful compromise. Maybe the person who's super invested in the holiday
can be the researcher and the other person will take control of
the financial aspect. Whatever the solution, work together and
show kindness to each other in the same way you would to your
neighbour or friend.

Differences in everyday values are one of the most common
problems couples face, and in the long run, they can be quite damaging if they are not in alignment. Bottling up your emotions is a
fast track to an even worse problem, so it's important to get it out in
the open and deal with the issue like adults. Whether it's renovation
materials, parenting, dishwashing or even food decisions, don't let
small value items turn into big value problems.

Most importantly of all, be timely with communicating your
grievances. Don't forget that respect and kindness is the foundation
of your flourishing relationship.

When 'I Do' Feels Like 'I Don't'

Most of us are familiar with the meaning of 'turning *on*' your partner, but as it turns out, 'turning *toward*' your partner is a lesser-known but considerably more important priority for connection. If you make a conscious effort to consistently turn towards your partner, you likely get to enjoy both! When that conscious effort is missing in action, it's more like you're both unconscious and the 'I do' feels like 'I don't'.

In any relationship, we seek emotional connection from our partners. This takes the form of distinct 'bids', as outlined by scholar Dr John Gottman.[29] These bids are related to gaining a sense of safety derived from attention, conversation, approval, sympathy, and play etc. Consider the following 'bids':

- 'Can you help me find my other sock?'
- 'Did you notice that Meghan Markle doesn't wear pantyhose?'
- 'How about that amazing goal in the third quarter?'
- 'What did you get up to today?'
- And the quintessential 'Does my bottom look big in this?'

All of these seemingly innocuous questions represent various attempts at making a connection in the form of interest, reassurance and emotional support.

How you respond to any one of these bids can be summarised as one of three 'turns':

Turn *against* your partner. When you respond to one of these attempts at connection with hostility. You snap at them and tell them you're busy or concentrating. You may even tell them to nick off with 'Shhhh, Johnny Depp is on the tellie!'

Turn *away* from your partner. You ignore or dismiss them. You might pretend you haven't heard, or maybe even give a little shrug to drive your apathy home. This is also a tactic commonly deployed after conflict.

> You actively engage with your partner's bid for attention. You look at them, respond and ask questions to show interest and empathy.

Turn *toward* your partner. Here it is! You actively engage with your partner's bid for attention. You look at them, respond and ask questions to show interest and empathy. 'Yes, your cheesecake is just as good as Sally's!' or 'Wow, that must have been so embarrassing. What did you do then?'

All interactions between couples have a mixture of these responses depending on life stressors such as health, work and sleep. Turning away, or even against your partner now and then isn't going to destroy a relationship. Couples who consistently turn toward each other, however, fare a lot better.

Gottman's research involved analysing married couples over six years. They found that those that were still happily together at the six-year mark 'turned toward' each other 87% of the time.[30] That's high, and still allows you some room for the occasional, 'Uh-huh. Very nice.' These couples were called the 'Masters'. By contrast, the couples who had fallen apart were labelled very bluntly as 'Disasters' and only managed to 'turn toward' and connect **three** times out of ten. *Ouch.*

Here's how can we strive to 'turn toward' our partners more often to give them as much engagement and attention as we're capable of:

Look for the positives. 'Masters' view their environment and their partners more appreciatively. They create an air of respect and gratitude for each another, making it easier to engage with the other person's bids for attention.

Disagree respectfully. 'Disaster' couples look at their lives and partners negatively. They get hung up on any failing, no matter how inconsequential, finding themselves tearing at each other disrespectfully as they enter the express elevator to separation. If you need to voice it, consider your delivery and use your 'feeling' words (such as hurt, disappointed, frustrated or embarrassed) to convey the impact of their behaviour. 'Helpful' in woman language can mean 'critical' in man language. Consider what outcome it is you want. A partner expressing their desires is always more powerful than debating or disagreeing with their spouse's thinking, which can be disrespectful. Consider the language you use. 'I would love it if...'. Take out the 'you'.

Understand why you argue. Many arguments stem from a sense of disconnection. It is not about the dishwasher or the toilet seat. It is about whether the other person has your back and supports you. Underneath our exterior we might fear abandonment, and that fear might turn to anger. This, in turn, causes us to lash out at the person we're terrified of living without. When you understand how insidious this fear of disconnection truly is, it's easier to put the effort into those 'bids' for connection.

Enjoy individuality. You and your partner are not clones! For all your similarities, you have different tastes and interests. Let your partner know how much something

Understanding the magnitude of acknowledging 'bids' builds a stronger relationship and once you actively start 'turning toward' your partner more regularly, that inevitably turns everything else ON as well!

means to you: they don't need to necessarily partake in everything you do, they just need to know that it is meaningful.

Be kind. If your partner is down in the dumps and you're tired and laid out on the couch, it can be the greatest gift in the world to get up and hold them tight. It's these small gestures, these small expressions of kindness and compassion, that exemplify turning towards your partner when they need it.

In most cases, turning *toward* your partner is simply what you would politely do to almost anyone, from your neighbour to your child's teacher or a good friend. Understanding the magnitude of acknowledging 'bids' builds a stronger relationship and once you actively start 'turning toward' your partner more regularly, that inevitably turns everything else ON as well! All say 'I do' to that!

Feedback or Criticism?

A quick show of hands: who likes criticism? If you raised your hand, I'm not *entirely* sure I believe you. Anyone who has been in a relationship can probably think of a few times when they've given their partner feedback only to have it explode in their face. Or, just as likely, been the one to blow up.

Or, *most* likely, done *both*.

In the same conversation.

Feedback is something that is always a *lot* easier to give than to receive, right? Let's take a look at a strategy you could use to make feedback easier to swallow. You can even try this on your boss!

The 'complaint sandwich' is a basic structure for your feedback (or criticism, complaint, gripe etc.) that will make it not only easier for the receiver to listen to, but is much more likely to inspire change. At the very least, it shouldn't explode in your face.

A complaint sandwich requires three ingredients:

- A positive statement
- The complaint
- A second positive statement

The biggest problem with receiving feedback in any area of our lives is feeling attacked. With the complaint sandwich, the meat of the problem is wedged between two positive comments, putting a structure around the complaint. This makes it feel less like a personal assault and more like, well, feedback. You start with something you appreciate about the situation or person and end with reassurance to calm both of your stress responses.

Now, if you're thinking to yourself, *great, next time he leaves the toilet seat up I'll just say 'Ben, you're a wonderful father, but if you leave the lid up again I will leave you, and beforehand burn everything you own. I really like what you've done with your beard'*, then I have some sad news. Yes, the complaint sandwich will make it easier to swallow, but no, you can't just say whatever you want in the middle. That would be like biting into a sandwich and finding a cockroach. It's still technically a sandwich, but you're not going to be terribly happy about it.

> Take responsibility for your own emotions. Avoid telling your partner what you think they are feeling ('you' talk) and speak about your feelings.

For the complaint sandwich to be effective and tasty, you do need to put some effort into making a filling that tastes good. Follow this recipe for a more palatable dish:

- **Prepare**

  Before you open your mouth, remember you're speaking to someone you 'love' (unless they are your boss?). Consider the outcome you're seeking.

- **One complaint at a time**

  A complaint sandwich is best as a toasted cheese sandwich. Not toasted cheese and ham or cheese and tomato or with that braised beef from the tin I like. Just cheese. Piling in multiple complaints together makes them all mash into one and contributes to the recipient feeling attacked. Stick to one issue at a time.

- **Make it timely**

  When they're already late for work or feeling under the

weather, it is not the best time to serve them up a 'You Snore Too Much' sandwich. Furthermore, avoid complaining about something that happened six months ago. You know very well the momentum a thought can get when you've stewed over it for way too long, easily boiling over into an unrelated conversation. Courageously approach them whilst it's still fresh in everyone's memory.

- **This is what I felt**

  Take responsibility for your own emotions. Avoid telling your partner what you think they are feeling ('you' talk) and speak about your feelings. For example, I feel hurt, happy, scared, frustrated etc. as compared to what you'd automatically want to say, 'You're lazy' or 'You don't seem to care.'

- **Keep it civil**

  Try to remain as calm and even-tempered as possible. Notice your tone, breathing, heart rate and any triggers from their expression. The goal of a complaint is to bring attention to an issue and try to get it resolved instead of trying to make them feel bad.

- **It is more about what they did**

  Separate the behaviour from the person. Describe exactly what you saw or heard and consider what video footage would have recorded. Keep it simple and don't make assumptions. For example, instead of 'You barged in in a huff and slammed the door', try 'I felt startled when I heard the door slam.'

- **This is the meaning it had for me**

  We all interpret and perceive things differently. By saying

'What I understood about this is…' it allows you to share your interpretation of the situation without accusing your partner.

- **Ask for what you need**
  You are entitled to respectfully make a clear request that would make you feel better. This also avoids making the person feel helpless as to what to do with your feedback.
- **Forgive**
  Once you've communicated your thoughts and feelings, then invite peace with forgiveness. You've done what you can to make the situation better and now it's time to let it go.

With these strategies, you'll be on your way to providing—and perhaps even receiving—much more palatable feedback in the future.

Two Words Relationship Therapists Wish They Could Say

The brave, beautiful couples who attend my sessions receive a gift. It is curated with love and presented only to those whom I know can handle and deserve it. This is gifted early in my clients' journey through sipping my vast selection of delicious teas in my beautiful sanctuary of an office.

What type of gift?

It is well thought out, personalised and can save you bucket loads of money that could be funnelled into your exotic travel plans, your children's education, their fanciful wedding or your retirement fund. It ingeniously saves you wasted time in court negotiations. The ruffled bow on top of the gift represents the ripple effect on generations to come who will be impacted by the important decisions you make during this tough phase in your life.

This gift is an analogy for my warm but stern 'Make sure you TRI'ed Bonding concept; presented with enough passion and love, it's enough to ruffle even the burliest, tattooed fly-in-fly-out miner!

The gift card features my powerful 'tell it how it is' dialogue designed to remind the couple why they initially signed up for this relationship. The fruits of this gift can be passed down as a legacy, particularly for those with children. I'm not professing to be a prophet with a mysterious message, however, it's the gift of the confronting truth of not trying hard enough! This is of course delivered in the format of a 'feedback sandwich', highlighting the couple's strengths, dishing out the tough love part then encouraging the couple to hope for change like many successful dynamos before them.

You are a relationship mentor whether you have children or not! It's worth considering the extended complications when you re-partner, throw step-children in the mix and likely bring your old habits to your next relationship. Innumerable clients who have married multiple times tell me they regret not trying harder.

Speaking of mentors, some of us can blame our grandparents or even parents for ill-equipping us! Whilst we can't directly 'sock it to them', our ancestors were less likely to require wisdom on how to collaborate with their spouse in areas such as finances and how to raise the children. They didn't need to check in with each other as their relationships featured more clearly defined, traditional roles that didn't overlap so much. This is in comparison to today's common tag team situation—symptomatic of both couples working outside the home—where we collide on work, home duties and parenting decisions.

If you're also thinking you're in the 'chose poorly and made a ghastly mistake' basket, perhaps suffering maltreatment from a partner with substance abuse issues, controlling family members or nasty narcissistic behaviours to name a few, this gift is likely not going to solve

> ... today's common tag team situation—symptomatic of both couples working outside the home—where we collide on work, home duties and parenting decisions.

things for you. Whilst some of those challenges can be overcome, you deserve to enjoy a partnership founded on respect and kindness. Don't allow the fear of being alone or of an uncertain financial situation to inhibit your safety and well-being.

There are hundreds of happiness studies including the longest study of young men from Boston that commenced in 1938.[31] Whilst these young men professed to pursue money and fame to be happy, the results were unexpected and I enjoy warm goose bumps every time I think about it. Make sure you look that one up on YouTube as this is an example of why I keep turning up at work each week!

Close relationships keep people happy. They help buffer life's challenges, delay mental and physical decline and are the biggest predictor of a long and happy life. Your social class, level of intelligence or genes aren't going to forecast bright skies and sunshine in your life, however, your satisfying significant other will certainly be there with an umbrella.

This, my reader, is promise enough for you to pursue a dynamic and flourishing relationship and for me to turn up to support clients in the counselling room again tomorrow. Over a thousand clients have benefitted from my gift which features a simplistic strategy of how to TRI Bonding. It's all there for the taking, that is—if you can push beyond your human tendency to protect your ego and win. No one wins then.

I'm giving this gift to you, should you wish to accept it.

How hard should you both try at fixing your relationship?

Harder.

What are the two words relationship therapists wish they could say?

Try Harder.

How can you both win?

I say—'TRY BONDING'.

TRI Bonding

Step 1 - Be a genius

Whilst you can reveal all your personality traits from oodles of analysis tools such as Myers Briggs, DISC, Enneagram, Winslow, Holtzman Inkblot and Energy profiling, one first step is to stop trying to make your partner a carbon copy of you and of your way of doing things. Relish the ingenious idea that everyone is a piece of a puzzle in your world designed to complement you. You likely were attracted to this person because they were different from you. The greatest aspect of this gift is to accept that you partnered with your spouse because their different quirks were endearing, they complemented you and you appreciated those gushy, 'Meeeee too' moments.

Step 2 - Track your conflict cycle

Be aware of your feelings, body sensations and behaviours during your same old dance routine from which you swap out topics. Couples often find it helpful to seek a relationship expert for their unbiased, without emotion clarity and birds-eye view to help unveil what they're doing. You're likely to have curated some repetitive pursue-withdrawal dance steps designed to propel you toward pleasure and away from pain—usually unsuccessfully. You can also read more on Dr Sue Johnson's contribution to this step in Toolbox Topic Six.

Step 3 - Forgive

It's an important phase of relinquishing the toxic seeds that only enliven your body's natural stress response versus calming it to invite healthy relationships. Forgiveness only requires *one* person—you! We covered more on the 'How to' in Toolbox Topic Two.

Step 4 - Draw a triangle

This is where you can lean on the most robust shape in the world! Now for some geometry. **The triangle is the strongest geometric shape.** Triangles are very hard to distort from their normal shape because of their fixed angles and ability to distribute force evenly to the other sides. Even force! That's what we're aiming for. Even better—a united force to be reckoned with. Your triangle stands securely with an arched banner over the top, emblazoned RESPECT AND KINDNESS. It's a good idea to draw that in as well because chances are, it fell down around the same time as the sun set on sexual intimacy. And it's highly likely that *that* only returns when it's a full moon, the stars are aligned and quite possibly alcohol is involved. (See diagram on next page)

Your behaviour in the triangle reflects this understanding of respect and kindness that helped hook you into each other when you first met! Now those cute quirks you found so endearing and fascinating at the beginning are grating and repetitive.

The 'you always' negativity sets in like heavy cement in your relationship and you're unable to chip your way out even with the sharpest words shovelled back and forth.

For every time you disagree, you could be seeking to deepen your connection with greater understanding instead. You would then be propelling your relationship to far greater depths of intimacy. It's truly magical to watch a couple constructively use conflict and adapt themselves in order to consider each other's needs, resulting in a beautiful new aligned

TRI BONDING

Respect and Kindness

Partner 1

Partner 2

Baseline where couples usually get stuck!

Back and forth. No one wins.

Questions

TURN TOWARD

Questions

Questions

REMAIN RESPECTFUL

Questions

Inquisition

INQUISITION

Inquisition

END RESULT - HE/SHE GETS ME!
WHEN YOU BOTH 'TRI BONDING'

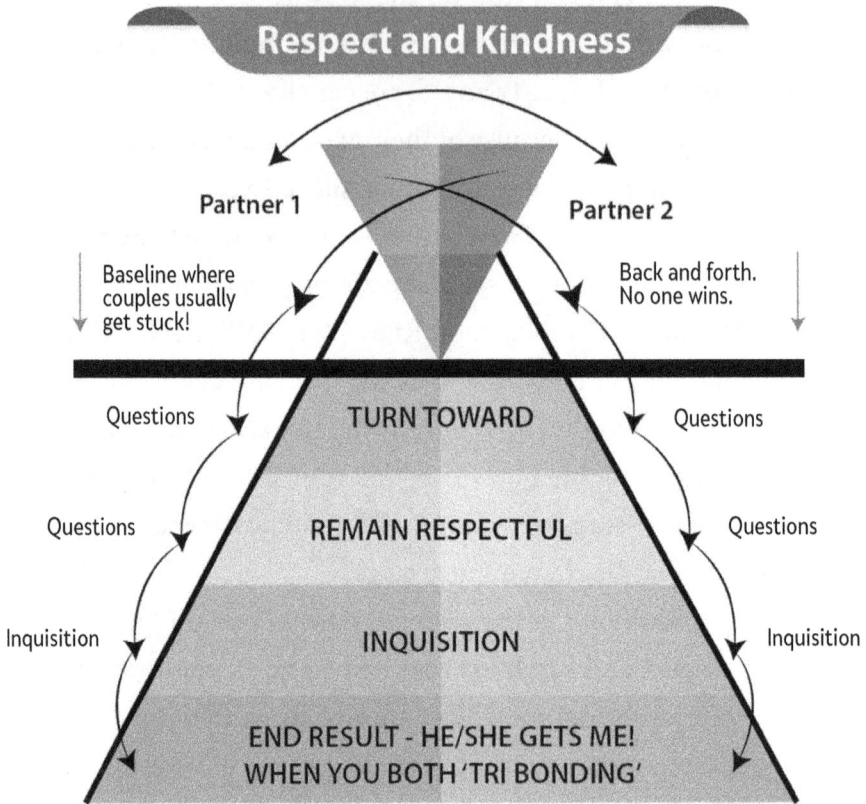

partnership. You won't always agree, however respectfully considering each other as you approach that same topic next time, when you've aligned yourselves, is another thing.

If you place yourselves on either side of the triangle of your disagreement, most couples will hover around the top of their triangle attempting to navigate their way out with a win.

For example:

Fred, 'You're always late. It's so rude.'

Freida, 'No, I'm not. What about my parent's wedding anniversary you turned up late for?'

Fred, 'I was working, and you knew I had to submit a proposal.'

Freida, 'Don't point the finger at me then.'

Back and forth like table tennis. Except someone can win at table tennis. Not so much in this instance.

Here's how you can regain that rapport, friendship, support and unconditional compassion and start to appreciate each other again:

Step 5 - Start TRI'ing on your point of difference

In the centre of your triangle, write this:

Turn Toward

Remain Respectful

Inquire

Some wonderful influencers in the relationship field include doctors Julie and John Gottman who coined this term of '**turning toward**' each other in recognising each other's 'bids for connection', which we covered earlier in this chapter.

You're asked to be acutely aware of '**remaining respectful**' in your line of questioning and answering. Avoid sarcasm, rolling of the eyes, and turning your query into a defensive attack.

Allow at least 15 minutes of one-sided and uninterrupted '**inquiry**' time that allows one partner to work down their partner's side of the triangle. This is a genuine line of questioning seeking to provide the gift of being in the other's shoes. You could even name it a respectful inquisition which aims to gain the truth of the matter through investigation.

If your inquiry involves learning more about the criticism being dealt to you—such as why your dishwasher stacking process is not acceptable—then know that it's naturally excruciating to contemplate seeking to know more about your deficiencies. Defy your human nature to protect your ego and your sense of rightfulness. Ask more questions. Don't know what else to ask?

> Lean in and find out what it's like to be your partner for a change. It will be a weird and wildly wonderful experience.

Try:

'Tell me more'.

'What would you have liked to happen instead?'

'How could this be done differently in the future?'

Lean in and find out what it's like to be your partner for a change. It will be a weird and wildly wonderful experience. You're probably used to hovering around the top of the triangle entrenched in your habit of 'pass the ball back and forth'. You are equally determined to win, that is, until that ball drops you both into the pain and isolation of slammed doors, screaming, silence or whatever your 'conflict ball game' looks like. I've seen plenty of these routines in my life and they tend to be so well-rehearsed that you'll need to be patient with yourselves to unlearn it! The key here is to self-compassionately recognise that these are your best attempts to cope, then shelve your innate desire to retort with defensiveness or attacks. Avoid defaulting to all those reasons why your partner is completely wrong until it's your turn to enjoy being on the receiving end of the respectful inquisition. 'BONDING' elements support your process.

B - Bare your soul. Recognise your inherent relational design that thrives on harmony and connectedness through being vulnerable. We all long to be heard, valued and respected so lose the ego and humbly approach this opportunity for feedback.

O - Open your ears. Use them in direct proportion to the one mouth you've been gifted! Be an active, emotionally attentive participant. Avoid distractions or appearing bored and apathetic. Use eye contact. When you're flooded with emotion and can't hear, then recognise that you need to take time out.

N - Non-Judgementally reflect and clarify what you're hearing without sarcasm—genuinely reflect words to ensure your correct understanding.

D - Discipline. The effort required to control your heightened emotions when you are triggered by hearing feedback you don't like is enormous!

I - Invest in this time with your partner and understand what it's like to be in their shoes with their opinion right now.

Leave your protests, retorts and attacks under your tongue. Shelve them until it's your turn!

N - **Nurture** your partner's position with empathy. Despite the odds, entertain their perspective, contemplate and wonder.

G - **Gift** your partner with being an active participant!

The magic transpires when you've gone so far down to the base of your partner's triangle that they start to feel, *'They get me! I have hope'*. Even if you're still disagreeing, at least you're talking about precisely what is going on.

I suspect that when you get trapped in the top of the triangle, you're usually arguing over assumptions made from a few keywords that set you off!

Swap over—allow the equal amount of time for your partner to respectfully give you the inquisition.

The awesome thing is, you can still disagree about who left the gate open and let the dog out after you've TRI'ed

> For renovating relationships, as you practise TRI'ing Bonding, look ahead and anticipate common challenges and collisions in your household.

Bonding. You're now at a place of deeper understanding and likely closer to the root cause which may be fear, lack of self-worth or grief. The exciting moment I love watching is empathy and collaboration at the bottom of the triangle. It usually features, 'I didn't know you felt this way', 'I didn't mean to put you in that position,' 'I honestly didn't know that about myself.' It's beautiful to see the zapping of the connection!

You know you've TRI'ed Bonding when you are at peace, knowing that you gave this concept and your relationship your all. Whatever the outcome, you can contentedly relay to your children at their 21st birthday, on their wedding day, at the birth of their children and beyond that your decision to TRI Bonding was the best thing you ever did. Even if you couldn't save your relationship, you cannot have regret, because you have peace knowing that you pulled out all the stops with respect and kindness. This strategy is worth using in *any* relationship. It is equally important to recognise that sadly it may not save *every* relationship—sometimes in abusive or one-sided situations the healthiest thing to do is to move on.

For renovating relationships, as you practise TRI'ing Bonding, look ahead and anticipate common challenges and collisions in your household. Collaboratively create strategies for roles, responsibilities, screen usage etc. Be specific about it. This can include the whole family. I highly recommend TRI'ing Bonding on fun topics such as holidays, ice cream and movies to normalise your respectful inquisition and set yourselves up for any tricky topics ahead. Have fun with this! I'd love to respond on an inquisition as to why *Footloose* is better than *Dirty Dancing*.

Nail this, and you launch yourselves to success as that super dynamic loving and connected duo that others admire and learn from for generations to come!

TAKEAWAY TOOLS

It doesn't matter what the conflict is about; how you use your communication skills to convey *how you're feeling about it* does matter. A lot!

- Our incredible mix of mosaic masculine and feminine brains differ in the way they communicate. More masculine brains get to the point quickly, more feminine brains require detail and emotion to get the point across. Be patient, you will get to the crux of the point sooner (without detail) or later (with lots).
- Couples must communicate with each other if there is a point of contention. Don't, and I'll see you at my practice sooner or later.
- Every bit of communication is important. Turn toward your partner as they make bids for your attention and express your interest. Watch your relationship blossom.
- Communicate your conflict with feedback, not criticism. The complaint sandwich is an excellent tool to make the things you dislike about your partner easier for them to hear and act upon… and vice versa.
- Learn and use my TRI Bonding method to help you gain a greater understanding of your partner and why they think and act the way they do. Opening the lines of communication and being willing to work through to the

root cause of arguments could save you and your family from a lot of heartache.

- Many relationship therapists wish they could say 'TRI Harder' and I would be negligent if I didn't!
- If separation is imminent, TRI Bonding can still make the 'uncoupling' process a smoother and more harmonious transition.

Renovate Your Relationship

MAINTENANCE

Make maintaining your relationship intentional and regular, not just as a one-off this week. There are plenty of ways to keep the wheels of your relationship turning smoothly, it just takes a little effort from you both.

Why Your Relationship Is Like Riding a Bike

Now that you're TRI'ing Bonding and nailing healthy conflict behaviours more frequently, your relationship renovation requires maintenance memory. What does your memory have to do with a thriving and dynamic relationship? I'm not talking about mistakenly calling your boyfriend by your ex's name or getting in trouble for forgetting your anniversary. This is about keeping your relationship in your explicit memory versus your implicit memory. I love the contribution from renowned clinician Stan Tatkin for his analogy of how your implicit memory knows how to ride a bike and you don't consciously think about it.[32] This might be where you've allowed your relationship to be chugging along right there in the background. You know the spokes are rotating day-in day-out without effort but you've also noticed that they're getting rusty. The squeaky whining of your neglected bike is gradually becoming louder and worse till the brakes fail as you career out of control down a steep mountain towards the deep dark valley of 'Splitsville'.

Compare this to explicit memory, where matters are intentionally recalled daily. Your bike is lovingly and regularly maintained with attention given to keeping those fine curves and strong frame polished and the chains well lubricated. It is one that others admire; they might even wish they had one like it. Even your children watch how you lovingly maintain it, learning through observation how to care for their bikes too.

So, what to do with a rusty, creaky bike? You take a good explicit look at what it needs. You might head to the bike shop for some advice, maybe a new pump, extra tools and some free strategies from the friendly bike store person who expertly recognises the importance of maintaining your bike to both save you money and save you the effort of going to look for a new one. Alternatively, if you decide it's just too much trouble, that same friendly bike store person gets to take your well-earned cash and helps you to buy a bike knowing you will likely end up back there in the same dilemma a year or three down the track.

Pop it into the forefront of your mind and your explicit memory! How do you do that? Make maintaining your relationship intentional and regular, not just as a one-off this week. There are plenty of ways to keep the wheels of your relationship turning smoothly, it just takes a little effort from you both. The good news is that most of the maintenance 'schemes' are very enjoyable for both partners!

If you feel like your bike requires a tune-up, first find out exactly where that care and attention is needed within your relationship; complete my quiz at www.relationshiprejuvenator.com/statusquiz to kick-start your maintenance towards relationship success.

When you're both back on a roll, ensure you're in alignment by regularly checking in with your partner, aligning with each other's needs, challenges, hectic schedules, parenting styles and forward planning.

Misalignment may occur when:

- Partners aren't growing at the same pace in critical areas of their life that adjust their perspective of the relationship.
- A frantic pace of life exists and little time is set aside for face to face communication.
- Poor communication skills abound.
- External family influences reinforce differing values and opinions.

I realise you can't anticipate every step of life together; however, it is worth having a decent crack to avoid constantly falling into the potholes of misalignment.

Why does your mechanic check the wheel alignment of your vehicle? It avoids unnecessary wear on your tyres, steering, suspension and brakes. The keyword here is 'unnecessary'—why would we drift apart unnecessarily without harmonising each other's sexual flavours, spirituality, personal development, goals and dreams?

There are a number of other highly recommended tools I use in my practice for self-maintenance and alignment, including the well-researched online analysis tool 'Prepare/Enrich', scientifically proven to improve your dynamics and relationship skills.[33] I use this instrument for everyone from pre-marriage couples and post-marriage one-year check-ups through to highly conflicted couples on the brink of entering that dreaded and expensive 'Splitsville'. Here, each partner completes a tailored set of questions online that takes about 30 minutes and we then go through the report together over a number of weeks (the blokes especially appreciate the charts and graphs!). There's even a simpler couple check-up version you can do yourself today.

Couples who take the time to review their relationship have the potential to reduce their chance of divorce by 30%. It's quite novel to examine your relationship dynamic and your personality style and find new constructive dialogues to set you up for success.

Another wonderful clinician tool I use is the Gottman Relationship Check-up.[34] It is facilitated by trained practitioners and provides yet another level of depth with 480 questions about everything from friendship to intimacy. You rate yourself on how well you

> ... you would never grease and polish just one wheel on your bike, leaving the other to rust and fall apart. Maintaining your relationship is the task of both spouses.

know your spouse, how you manage emotions and conflict, share your values and goals, and what gives meaning to your lives. There's not much it doesn't cover about parenting, housework, finances and trust and you also then learn new healthy conflict cycles that can be a positive example to others around you!

Don't be afraid of the findings from these analyses; they are not meant to give a pass/fail score, but rather a health check-up like the one you'd get from the bike mechanic when he looks at what level of maintenance is needed to get a smooth ride going again. You *can* turn around a substandard and conflicted relationship that's hurtled out of control. It is never too late to begin and it's worth the effort as a couple to invest the time in these tools versus experiencing the angst in investing in your lawyer. And remember, you would never grease and polish just one wheel on your bike, leaving the other to rust and fall apart. Maintaining your relationship is the task of both spouses.

You can read more about these analysis tools at:

www.relationshiprejuvenator.com/pre-marriage-education.

What to Do With Free Gifts With Purchase

'I really do have a soft spot for my mother-in-law. It's out in the garden behind the garage,' said one client recently as she chuckled guiltily.

Did you hear about the office administrator who said, 'Hey, boss, can I have a day off next week to visit my mother-in-law?' 'Certainly not!' the boss replied. The office guy says, 'Thank you so much. I knew you would be understanding.'

One last one. 'I haven't spoken to the mother-in-law for six months now ... apparently, it's rude to interrupt.'

You guessed it; the focus is mothers-in-law. I'll cut the jokes now as I'll likely be one myself in time.

This isn't just about the outlaws, but extended family and friends too.

Starry-eyed romantics are often caught unawares after slipping into the love vortex. Clarity is skewed thanks to oxytocin—the love neurochemical that helps us pair up. Many seal their commitment with a kiss and a ring, only to realise down the marital track there's a whole new group of influencers behind their beloved.

There's Uncle Bert who drops in unannounced way too often and yet your spouse seems incredibly nonplussed. How about your partner's best friend you've never really gelled with from the start? Ever heard of that inappropriate sister-in-law who reveals way too much about your partner's ex? Do you have a father-in-law who unashamedly runs a dictatorship around the money that you've earned? Speaking of your hard-earned coin, how are your stepchildren syphoning that out of your lifestyle? Then there's the wedding day—so many expectations for the most wonderful, memorable celebration. It's too often tainted by the bitter sadness of those family members who weren't included enough or managed to bustle their way in with far too much influence. This rather excruciating list could go on.

> There are so many challenges when it comes to the 'free gifts with purchase' extended family and friends. In my experience, the greatest conflict arises when you feel your partner prioritises them over you.

There are so many challenges when it comes to the 'free gifts with purchase' extended family and friends. In my experience, the greatest conflict arises when you feel your partner prioritises them over you.

Relationships become strained during those times when you long for your partner to 'have your back', but that support never comes, or when you feel as though you need them to protect and nurture you from the opinions or bizarre behaviours of others.

When we talk about culture, it must be noted that you and your spouse could have been raised in the same street in Sydney and yet still experience significant cultural family differences, as if one of you was from Saudi Arabia and the other Tasmania.

What to do?

Firstly, let's assume that anyone unlike yourself is just, well, weird. Those people who may stray from your ideals, values and behaviours are aliens. Your in-laws will often fall into this category. Your partner's nuances and behaviours are super cute at the start. When a few of those start to grind on you, there's that shocking revelation! With utter dismay, you realised there's a couple with frighteningly similar habits who just happen to live on the planet your partner came from. You exclaimed, 'You're just like your mother (or father)!' How did that go down? I know. Not so well.

Many find that in order to cope they've built themselves a quiet place inside their imaginary cave as a last resort. Others are still feisty and will attack any outsiders who may compromise the new family culture they're trying to create. Thankfully, from this point forward you will now be better equipped to handle these situations using the following tips that form the acronym RESPECT.

R - Respect. Everyone deserves it and so do you. You are likely different from your in-laws, but it's important to respect the parents of the spouse you've chosen to love. The level of involvement with them that is healthy for you and your relationship is another thing.

E - Establish boundaries that support your new family culture. You and your partner can decide what are the best and worst parts of your respective upbringings and determine which bits you'd like to bring to your own new family culture.

S - Set boundaries for those aspects of your life you're unable to compromise on. This allows you to be more patient and flexible to accept the differences in other

> What a beautiful gift to your partner to integrate their traditions or funny quirks into your lives for comfort and familiarity.

areas. What a beautiful gift to your partner to integrate their traditions or funny quirks into your lives for comfort and familiarity. Can you try and replicate that Chocolate Self Saucing pudding his mother used to lovingly make for your husband?

P - Prepare yourself for visits and holidays. Evaluate your self-talk to ensure it is loving and kind. If you're already ruminating over their negative behaviours and your past hurts and grievances while plotting revenge, it won't take much for you to be triggered and react less than favourably. Hurling a glass of red wine at your sister-in-law on her wedding will likely be something you'll regret.

E - Enjoy them! Again, you've bought into this relationship and you will be investing favourably for long term returns if you make it your business to find something to like about them. What fascinating differences can you learn more about and appreciate?

C - Champion admirable behaviour and skip the constant judgement. It's exhausting and taxing on your mental health. Your spouse's friends and family may not have table manners, have the courtesy to call before dropping-in, or know when to stop drinking (and the list goes on). Instead of cutting them out of your life, can you consistently mentor your values and teach your children? Maybe it'll catch on?

T - Take steps to forgive! A reminder again that choosing not to forgive their wrongs holds you in a vice-like grip of toxic stress due to consistently high levels of cortisol in your body—even if you don't realise it. Who wants to die young because of their mother-in-law? It's best she goes first.

The Five Love Languages

Have you ever gone to great lengths to display your affection and it falls flat? Ever tried to pay someone a compliment or do something kind and they either barely noticed or seemed unappreciative? Has someone even rejected your gesture? *'What was that about?'* you thought with dismay and hurt. You were probably quite confused as you would have loved it if someone had said or done that to you. *How could they be so rude?*

Have you done something wrong?

Don't take this too harshly but, yes, you probably did.

But not in the way you're thinking.

Everyone expresses and understands love differently. How we express it to others and how we accept it, differs from person to person.

This is called your love language and is certainly one of the many essential concepts in a marriage therapist's tool kit. It's simple and effective. I can't tell you how many clients have

> You must learn to speak each other's language so you both feel truly loved by one another.

told me they wished they knew about this for their 'first marriage'. You're welcome to read *The 5 Love Languages* book by Gary Chapman or take a shortcut and head to his website The5LoveLanguages. com to find out your love language within minutes.[35]

Whilst you'd think displays of affection would be universal, or at least generally consistent within a culture, you'd be wrong.

Every single person communicates love differently.

Every. Single. One.

Sure, there will be overlap. 'I love you' is rather straight forward and clearly understood by most people, however, we all have our little quirks and desires. These aren't just based on the culture and society in which we were raised, but influenced by our upbringing and experiences as well.

I'm here to shine the light bulb on yours, to check you don't spend the rest of your next or current relationship either flying at a different altitude or in a completely different direction to your partner!

Your love language isn't just verbal. Chapman suggests there are five types of love languages and we use different combinations. The five types are:

1. Words of Affirmation
2. Receiving Gifts
3. Acts of Service

4. Quality Time
5. Physical Touch

You might be someone who expresses love through words of affirmation and physical touch.

Your partner may communicate love through quality time and acts of service.

You must learn to speak each other's language so you both feel truly loved by one another. In this example, you need to learn how to express love through quality time and they need to learn how to use words of affirmation. As a start, I'm providing ten examples:

1. Words of Affirmation

- Thank you for doing the dishes/cleaning/taking out the rubbish etc.
- Your caring heart makes me so happy.
- You are so beautiful/my big hot spunk.
- Thank you for always being there for me.
- You're my best friend.
- I don't know what I'd do without you.
- You have the cutest [insert facial feature here]
- You're doing so great! Don't give up.
- You inspire me to do better.
- I'm here for you.

If you're in a relationship and this is your love language, it's important to tell your partner exactly what style of 'words' you feel most loved hearing? Acknowledging your work and achievements could fill up your 'love cup' in a heartbeat, whilst hearing about their incredibly alluring looks is important for the next person.

Now, be mindful of the value of intrinsic versus extrinsic affirmations. Pastor Matt Thiele reveals quite a gap in knowledge of this topic in his literature review, *Intrinsic Affirmation and Marriage Satisfaction.*[36] He states the difference as being: 'Intrinsic affirmation affirms a person's unchanging core value—their worth independent of their performance or achievements. Extrinsic affirmation focuses on changing attributes such as appearance or achievement.'[37] Pastor Matt concludes, 'So extrinsic affirmations may not always produce the warm feeling the giver may intend to convey! What is needed is regular affirmation of the other's deep unchanging intrinsic worth. This reduces the stakes in conflict, reduces defensiveness, and enables marriage partners to feel understood, truly valued for who they are. True intrinsic affirmations produce secure relationships.'

> What is needed is regular affirmation of the other's deep unchanging intrinsic worth. This reduces the stakes in conflict, reduces defensiveness, and enables marriage partners to feel understood, truly valued for who they are.

I had not considered this important difference and the likelihood of defensiveness in the face of rarely feeling truly valued for what matters. Your partner may not be aware of the significance of intrinsic affirmations and be unlikely to ask for compliments on their core value so here's a big tip—don't overlook their kind heart and unique, inspiring way of viewing the world as an example.

The next step is to think further about *how* you want to hear it. Is it through handwritten notes, lipstick on the mirror, Snap-Chat or text message? We are individually created and have preferences, so you may as well help your spouse with what you need to support your connection.

2. Acts of Service

The desire of people whose love language is Acts of Service is, to quote the iconic Elvis Presley, 'a little less conversation and a little more action'. It's not that they don't care for a few kind words or expect a personal attendant either. They place great value in doing something that needs to be done without being asked. To them, performing these actions is a greater display of care and affection than saying it.

This can create some obvious tension when you've got one partner who speaks in Words of Affirmation and another who speaks in Acts of Service. The trick is for *both* partners to learn how to talk to each other. The one who uses words must learn to use actions, and the one who uses actions must learn to use words. It can be quite uncomfortable at first, however with a little repetition and consistency—you'll both be crooning 'Burning Love' instead of 'There Goes My Everything'.

Acts of service are often about small gestures rather than, 'I waxed your car, cleaned the entire house, washed the hound dog, have your lobster thermidor in the oven, and filed your taxes; now let me take off your blue suede shoes.' That certainly wouldn't go astray…but the reality is much smaller in scope.

Here are some examples of Acts of Service that may have

your partner jump up and jive with love:

- Make the bed in the morning.
- Pack their lunch for work.
- Run a bath for them.
- Engineer them some uninterrupted time to watch a show, a sports match, or read a book.
- Take out the garbage.
- Deliver breakfast in bed on a weekend.
- Run an errand such as grab a prescription or pick up the dry cleaning.
- Iron their clothes.
- Do the dishes.
- Offer to be the designated driver the next time you go out.
- Research something for them that would make their home chores, work or next trip easier.
- Let them sleep in.

I'm certainly not suggesting you sell your soul to slavery. Do take the time, however, to notice what your partner may have been trying to perform for you all these years. Those Acts of Service could well be what they've been singing out for. Expect a 'Suspicious Mind' when you suddenly turn on their love language but assure them it's just because 'I'm Stuck on You'.

Is this your love language? Maybe you need to be assertive about telling your spouse how they can 'Love Me Tender?'

'It's Now or Never!'

3. Gifts

'All I want for Christmas is youuuuuuuuuu,' crooned no person whose love language is Gifts ever!

This can be perceived as one of the pricklier languages of the lot. You think kids enjoy Christmas day the most?

Ha! A person with a Gifts love language is experiencing levels of bliss and joy those small children with their cherubic faces and unspoiled optimism can only dream about. From someone who falls into this category, I can't tell you how over the moon I was when my husband bought me a pair of $12 rubber boots for an outdoor music concert. Little did I know how incredibly useful they were about to become when the event became deluged in a torrential monsoon.

When it comes to the Gifts love language, it's really, really important to try to get away from the mindset that the person is materialistic. Some people *are* materialistic, don't get me wrong. For the Gift person, it's more the time, thought and effort that goes into the gift that truly expresses the love than the thing itself. A small, thoughtful gift—say, something as simple as a pair of rubber boots or replacing the teapot you recently broke (I hope he's reading)—is a grander expression of love to them than an expensive bracelet they have no want or need for. (Okay I lie, I wouldn't refuse that either.)

A non-gift person might feel the pressure of 'the bigger, the better,' whereas the Gift person just wants to feel that you understand them and thought of them that day.

If you feel helpless having realised your partner falls squarely in this category, simply start with the thought, the love and the understanding, *not* the price tag. Knowing that it's the thought that truly does count and that this is not some tired cliché will go a long way to establishing a healthy relationship with your Gifts love language spouse.

If you know your partner is stressed, mix it with the Touch or Quality Time love language, perhaps doing something massage-related. Cards attached to presents allow you to use Words of Affirmation. Alternatively, profess your heart-felt love with some romantic prose when you hand over the present. How about two tickets to the cricket for you and your sporty lover?

A box of their favourite popcorn would even do it for some people!

Non-gift love language people can struggle with the thought they must buy presents all the time. This isn't true. Simply surprise and delight at random unexpected times or when they might need a lift the most. As a heads-up, please, please whatever you do—remember birthdays and anniversaries.

Your Gift love language spouse is likely lavishing you with presents to express their love. Think back over the last year at how many gifts you've received from them. You'll probably notice they're things you've valued, wanted, or needed. If you're not a Gift person, you're probably taking those presents for granted and don't register them as signs of affection. You might even think they're trying to placate you with gifts to avoid showing affection? I suspect every one of those gifts you've received was their way of saying, 'I love you; I listen to you, I know who you are, and I know what you need.'

So, please ignore Mariah Carey and her misleading lyrics

that some people 'don't want a lot for Christmas, there is just one thing they need, they don't care about the presents, underneath the Christmas tree.'(sic). Yes, they probably want you for their own…accompanied by your incredibly thoughtful gift behind your back.

> Would you agree that 90% of being married is simply yelling, 'What?' from other rooms in the house?

Make time to lovingly trawl the shops or internet for that unique special something and have it by their birthday or Christmas. No, you can't hire a buyer's agent for this one but certainly, feel free to secretly research with their friends or family. Still at a loss? Ask them what they like.

4. Quality Time

Would you agree that 90% of being married is simply yelling, 'What?' from other rooms in the house? You might even consider this as ticking off Quality Time with your partner. *Bom Bom.* Sorry, that doesn't cut it and I'm here to save you from relationship erosion, especially if it's your spouse's love language.

You might think an afternoon in the same house is Quality Time, however, it goes beyond just proximity. It's a concept that should include focus and attention and I mean talking to and engaging with each other about each other.

If this is the love language of your spouse, why is it important?

- Your partner wants to feel like your other half. Whatever activity you need to do today, they probably want to do it *with* you. Even things that might seem boring, like running errands, can be a bit special for a Quality Time partner simply because you're together.

- There are few things worse than having a half-focused conversation with someone whose love language is Quality Time. It'll hurt, hard. Avoid distracted conversation. Be present and engaged. Look up from your screen. It's kind and respectful.
- Your gift of maintaining interest in their life is more valuable than you imagine. Ask them how their day was, then do nothing but listen and give them your full attention.

As we discussed previously, the love language of Gifts isn't about the gifts as much as the thought behind them. In the same way, Quality Time for your partner may well be no more than sitting next to each other watching a movie. Make your partner feel loved by planning special hangouts for just the two of you. Why not carve out some time at least once a week to make a snazzy meal together and play question games. Or perhaps a game of tennis? That will rack up a heap of quality time credits, especially if you're both competitive. Video games even count if you're playing together.

Other types of Quality Time are:
- board games
- extreme sports, triathlon or gym training
- cooking lessons or food festivals
- art gallery or museum tours
- surfing

- dance classes
- house chores
- trivia nights
- motorcycling

If you're in a relationship, you wouldn't be the first couple to look at me blankly across the couch at this point (even after the explanation and suggestions above) and still be trying to find some common ground on Quality Time. Rest assured; I've taken it upon myself to make a huge list of fabulous date ideas. You'll find them amongst other awesome tips in my Relationship Rejuvenator workbook at www.relationshiprejuvenator.com/books.

5. Physical Touch

By now, you should have unveiled the mystery of what your partner is seeking from you. You've also hopefully discovered the ingenuity of being assertive in order to ask for what you need. If you have successfully received the simple message that it's important to step out of your own blue suede shoes and express your partner's love language, NOT yours—you've graduated. Easy!

> The longer I counsel couples, the more I realise that physical touch can be a deal-breaker. Nothing means more to someone whose primary love language is Physical Touch than a tender caress.

Um—No, not always.

Not if you have different love languages.

Especially if one of them is the fifth language of Touch!

Now I'm sure you'd like me to head straight south with this one. It is not, however, only about a bit of crumpet, doing the hibberty jibberty or hitting a home run.

The longer I counsel couples, the more I realise that physical touch can be a deal-breaker. Nothing means more to someone whose primary love language is Physical Touch than a tender caress. You may gift them all the fishing rods, 3D printers, fitness watches or bracelets you can afford next Christmas but nothing communicates love like physical touch.

> May I stereotype here to highlight that women with a Touch love language so appreciate the implicit version without the dread that it will always require 'benefits.'

Let's brainstorm on what physical touch could include: holding hands, hugging, kissing, back rubs, arm around the shoulder, leg on leg while watching TV, head on lap on a rug in the sunshine. Let's break it down further to 'explicit touch,' which could well be requesting your full attention for a luxurious back massage or a lead into some afternoon delight. 'Implicit touch' can be a momentary connection such as a pat on the shoulder or a cheeky slap on the bott-bott as you pass by.

May I stereotype here to highlight that women with a Touch love language so appreciate the implicit version without the dread that it will always require 'benefits.' Whilst this, too, is fabulous fun, it's important to send a message that says, 'You are more than my pleasure bunny and I love you for who you are.' Just sayin, fellas!

Touch will need to be featured in your transitions of hellos and goodbyes. It's worth having a chat about what you appreciate when leaving your partner if this is your love language. Enjoy the relief in knowing that if your partner appreciates touch, simply holding them tight instead of trying to conjure up all the right words will be plenty enough.

If you were raised in a culture that did not display affection in this manner, it can be rather uncomfortable. In fact, for some, it is disturbing, excruciating and even embarrassing in public! As with all new habits, practise. If you've found yourself in a relationship with someone with a Touch love language, they'll appreciate your efforts more than you can imagine.

If it's relevant, I highly recommend you check out all the resources on the Five Love Languages for Children and Teenagers. It'll give you a wonderful parenting heads up on soothing your child and ensuring you truly show them the love they crave. There's a Five Love Languages book for everyone including singles and military personnel!

Cliché Dates

Dating is an integral part of maintaining your relationship before, during and after children. I've had countless conversations in the counselling room where couples tried to recall the last time they had an uninterrupted conversation without work distractions, screens, noise and children whining. The outside world will always be a distraction from your spouse, which is why carving out time to be alone together is very, very important. You need to continually ensure the foundation of your relationship is nurtured and strengthened so it's in a secure, strong position to weather challenges and differences.

The concept of the clichéd date night might make you cringe, but there's an excellent reason why you should incorporate some form of it into your routine.

We've all seen them in movies and on TV, or read about them in novels—I'm talking candlelit dinners at a fancy European restaurant, walks on the beach, or dinner and a show. You've probably rolled your eyes at half of them. Here's the thing, clichés become clichés for a reason. Usually, they *are* so popular because people enjoy them. We might sit and wonder how something as uncreative as a romantic dinner at a French restaurant could make it into a multi-million-dollar movie, but when was the last time you had a romantic dinner at a French restaurant? The fact is, it's nice. It's fancy. It's unusual.

It's, well, romantic.

And it gives you something to talk about.

The fact is you don't need to engage in all those sentimental, cliché romantic tropes we've seen in countless movies, but just because something's a cliché doesn't mean it's bad. Give some of these date night ideas a try and you may just realise how much you enjoy being with your spouse, regardless of the cliché:

- A walk in the park. There are some beautiful parks around, and quite a few that are well-lit at night time for a special pre- or post-dinner walk.
- Dinner and a movie. You can even combine the two by going

to a Gold Class cinema if there's one nearby so that you can have your cake and eat it too. Enjoy a beverage with it. Seek out an old school drive-in cinema for extra novelty.

- Candle-lit dinner. The ultimate cliché, yes—and that's the point!
- A trip to the beach. Soak up the sun during the day or enjoy a cool ocean breeze and the sand between your toes on a starry night.
- Even if you have small children, you still have plenty of opportunities to pop the children to bed, light the candles and make something simple or call in takeaway.

The possibilities are endless and you don't need to look too far for ideas, just download my workbook at www.relationshiprejuvenator.com/books. Try to get as corny and cringe-inducingly cliché as you can; take the bull by the horns and enjoy the time with your partner having the cheesiest fun possible. At the very least, you'll have something to talk about!

Communication Lubrication

You've hooked up, got hitched, produced heirs and been together for what feels like a thousand years. The kids have left home, (well, for now anyway) you're out for a nice dinner and suddenly, you have nothing to talk about!

We all know why: for the last couple of decades, any nights out were spent talking about all the things your darling cherubs had been up to, their amazing attributes and how they drove you crazy.

'Did you see that cute family drawing little Benny made featuring our ginormous ears?'

'What about the time Ashlee decided to use a crayon to create artwork on the walls to make the house look pretty?'

And all too soon it becomes:

> There are lots of reasons couples stop talking, the most common being that the longer you know someone, the easier it is to not bother to 'lean-in', enquire and talk.

'How do we stop Franny using SnapChat in her bedroom?'

'Do you think Johnny took $20 from my wallet?'

Now that those cherubs have grown up and moved out of home, you realise you've got not much more than...

'So ... how about the weather?'

Ugh.

There are lots of reasons couples stop talking, the most common being that the longer you know someone, the easier it is to not bother to 'lean-in', enquire and talk. At the start of the relationship, you've got a few decades of information to catch up on. You stay up all night talking and exploring each other's pasts and histories. The love drug oxytocin is flowing, eye contact is high and finding out what the other was doing before the date is fresh and exciting information. Then it's one, five, 10, or 20 years later and you realise you've run out of content. You've lost the drive to explore. You already know what they were doing before the date; they were getting ready.

You know. Because you were there.

Ugh.

Now in most cases, this lack of exploration isn't actually about losing interest in the other person (and when it is…well, that's a whole other chapter); it's just that neither person can honestly think of what to ask. They just need a little push in the right direction. So, push I shall! Here are some tips for reigniting conversation when your communication has run dry:

Revisit the past.

This might be your shared history or your respective upbringings. Recall those vivid memories of your best moments; maybe it was a whirlwind holiday across multiple countries, or just the first time you curled up on the couch together during a thunderstorm and watched TV. Why not pull out all those old photos from your childhood and laugh at your ridiculous hairstyles and your parents' fashion choices from when you were 10 years old. That *never* gets old and it helps add a few bricks to your 'safe relationship' house by sharing memories.

Discuss the little things.

Don't ever forget the small stuff. See something interesting? Point it out. See a puppy? Talk about why you never got a dog as a child or why you might like to be a wildlife volunteer one day. In the previous chapter, I discussed the importance of acknowledging your spouse's 'bids' for emotional connection. It's the little things in life that may not necessarily prompt the most profound conversation topics, but they do keep the conversation flowing. These momentary touches of connection have a greater impact than you realise.

Discuss difficult things.

At some stage everyone experiences fears, concerns and perceived shortcomings. Do you know what's great? Discussing them with your partner. It can be hugely mutually beneficial to not just simply air your worries, but to get feedback and reassurance. Honest feedback also goes under this umbrella. Nobody gets anywhere if you spend your relationship assuring each other that everything's fine when you wished that the other person would just, for once, chew with their mouth closed. All you achieve is getting riled up and one day exploding in frustration.

> The key is emotional attentiveness—that is, turn toward your partner and make an effort! You just never know where a little 'communication lubrication' might lead to.

Contemplate the future.

Is there a plan for your next five years of togetherness? Do you have interesting short-term personal goals to share? Happy couples discuss their futures. Making sure you both have complementing plans can prevent a lot of drama.

'I thought we were travelling the world on a sailing boat?'

'But I always wanted to settle down on a farm!'

Might want to sort that out quick smart. Why not talk about it?

So that's just a start! There are world events, community involvement, the environment, politics, sport and the arts. You will also find a plethora of resources on my website including Conversation Starters in my workbook at: www.relationshiprejuvenator.com/books.

Importantly, carve out a moment in time without distraction from any children, family or friends and turn toward each other. Use eye contact and intentionally engage to be present and open to possibilities and ask one or more of the following questions for an authentic conversation. I know some will be tempted to uncomfortably retort with ridiculous and humorous answers but try also to be real and genuine for this time you've set aside, precious minutes and hours intended for closeness and connection:

- What do you want less of this year?
- What do you long for?
- What has been the biggest drag for you this year?
- What are you dreaming about most right now?
- How can I help you this week?
- How do you describe me to people who haven't met me?
- What are your favourite ways to spend time with me?
- When were you last truly happy? What happened?
- What is the best way I can show you I love you this coming year?
- How can we unite to impact our world with more kindness?

If there are responses or ideas you don't agree with, enquire further and deepen your understanding instead of attempting to defend or shut down. I can't count the number of brave blokes that reveal that they struggle with the right responses for their adoring female who yearns to connect and share. Meanwhile, her words flow freely and easily and with magnitude! The key is emotional attentiveness—that is, turn toward your partner and make an effort! You just never know where a little 'communication lubrication' might lead to. Special thanks to one of my male clients, who came up with this rather apt term for what he needed to do more often and for my explanation for the positive results when you get it right!

The Fine Art of Accepting Compliments

Now that you've got the conversation flowing, what if you received a compliment along the way?

For me, I love compliments: there's nothing I like better than positive reinforcement to rock my world. It could be that lovely Helen from the local pool told me she read and liked my recent newspaper column, my husband said I look really pretty in that dress or my boys exclaimed that the spag bol I made is amazing. I just want to do a massive 'Oh What a Feeling' jump (refers to a popular advertising campaign) on those days. I then find myself generating even more tributes to others too. It has a ripple effect!

> Some of us have developed many reasons to deflect compliments, including a lack of self-acceptance from low self-esteem, shame and guilt, anxiety, depression, perfectionism and narcissism.

Yet so many of us at times in our life have enormous difficulty and feel incredibly awkward receiving the *verbal* gift of a compliment. It's no different to my best friend carefully selecting a well thought out *physical* gift, perhaps a book from my favourite author, and wrapping it beautifully. Imagine she excitedly presents it to me and I despondently say, 'No thanks, take it back.' What the heck? How hurt and disappointed would she be?

Some of us have developed many reasons to deflect compliments, including a lack of self-acceptance from low self-esteem, shame and guilt, anxiety, depression, perfectionism and narcissism. We can suffer some real hard-knocks and make some ridiculous choices in quick succession and spend the next few years emotionally beating ourselves up over them. Some people were raised hearing the theme '*You'll never be good enough*'. No wonder then, that you'd have trouble believing there's something worthwhile to say about the person you so often dislike—you. We go to great lengths to deflect compliments through denying them, arguing the case, diluting them, insulting ourselves in response or transferring the credit to someone else. Some even question the sincerity of the compliment giver.

You *know* you secretly relish the thought of praise for that delicious lemon cake you made, the new contract you signed off at work or for scaling that local mountain five times in a row. Yet it can be almost overwhelming to think that others think it's a big deal too, so how can we learn to enjoy and receive the gift of a compliment instead of deflecting or diluting it?

The Australian Institute of Professional Counsellors[38] suggest we try these ideas instead:

- Smile graciously, return eye contact, and say, 'Thank you.'
- Relax and breathe: it might be uncomfortable at the start, but intentionally breathe your way through it as you gain confidence.
- Add some additional relevant intel: 'Thanks, I got the recipe from…'

- Avoid a 'boomerang' compliment in return; this may seem insincere and de-values the gift you've just been given.
- Value-add: After your 'Thank you', convey your appreciation for the compliment to them.
- Be honest and optimistic. So what if your praised project isn't finished? Don't focus on what it's not yet, but what it will be.
- Ask a question. Why not genuinely ask specifically what they like about your outfit?
- Practice dishing out compliments: intentionally notice the wonderful attributes in others and share it in a timely fashion. They'll likely remember it for a long, long time.

Here's your first chance to practice: 'I love how you've got this far through the book!'

A Kiss and a Hug for Every Day of the Month

Birthdays, christenings, weddings, whatever the reason—for the vast majority, it means families, food…and hugs. Lots and lots of hugs. Baby hugs. Grandparent hugs. Then there's the Christmas hug season…hugs galore for months on end. For some of us, this is great! Most people like hugging. My clients even hug me. Some like longer hugs, some like shorter. Some like firm bear hugs,

> After a nice, six-second hug, your body releases some feel-good hormones and you feel more connected to the person you just held.

others like the accompanied air kiss, or the opposite of that. But whatever their shape or form, the consensus is that hugs are fantastic.

Then there are the other people. Those who dislike hugs, or actively avoid them. We all know one and you'd expect that they thrived throughout social distancing during the 2020 pandemic. Maybe you're one of them. For them, all those huggy holiday and high days are an unending nightmare of invaded personal space and drooling infants.

Whether you love them or hate them, hugs are a part of our lives. It turns out that they're more than a pleasant/annoying traditional greeting or show of affection: they are actually, pleasantly, good for your health.

Feelings of love are created through a cocktail of chemicals and hormones in the brain and body. One of the big ones is oxytocin. Oxytocin makes you feel good and makes you feel connected with other people and guess what? Hugs release oxytocin. The research results on the exact length you need to hug someone to enjoy a shot of oxytocin seems to vary from five to seven seconds, so I like to split the difference and just say six. After a nice, six-second hug, your body releases some feel-good hormones and you feel more connected to the person you just held. Even if we don't know the science behind it, we intuitively know that physical closeness makes us feel more connected. The role of oxytocin is complex, but there's increasing evidence to prove a number of other health benefits. Oxytocin, commonly referred to as the 'love drug':

Boosts the immune system

The presence of oxytocin increases other hormones that fight off infection. Simply by feeling love and connection with your fellow human beings, you are better at fighting off diseases.

Relieves pain
Got a headache? Hug someone! It might not be quite as effective as a pain relief pill but could well decrease your overall discomfort.

Lowers the risk of heart disease
Oxytocin can help reduce blood pressure, which in turn lowers the risk of heart disease.

Lowers social anxiety
Those with social anxiety would generally consider a hug the last thing they want in a social environment but it's probably the first thing they should get! A hug at the start of a social event can even make them feel more relaxed and open, rather than shy and anxious.

Deepens relationships
Depending on which is your Love Language, hugs are your soul food. You'd recall that for some people, touch is an incredible way to express and understand love. Take a moment to hug your partner every time they come home after all those long hours at work. Just six seconds out of your day to rest, recharge, and connect with your loved one is all you need to help de-stress, relax and reaffirm your love.

> During the act of kissing, we share genetic and immunological information and measure up our potential partners on a deeply biological level. How ... sexy?

Helps mothers bond

Oxytocin is released during childbirth and breastfeeding. Not only does it create strong bonds between adults, but it also helps create and strengthen the connection between mother and child. The relaxing element of oxytocin also makes breastfeeding easier.

Reduces stress and helps you sleep better

Relief from anxiety, social bonding and resilience to disease combine to lead to a reduction in your overall stress levels and improved ability to sleep.

All from a hug.

Take a moment to appreciate all the benefits your overenthusiastic family member is about to give you with their warm embrace. Now imagine the benefits of hugging someone you've chosen to spend your life with. The good part is that you can accompany it with a kiss!

How do you like kissing? It is awesome (according to me) and there are so many reasons to talk about it including that it's an exciting extension to a hug and could change your life in a moment, just like in the film *Sliding Doors*!

In our society, we place a lot of importance on kissing, but it's worth noting that we have no real idea as to why. Not every culture and society on Earth does it and nobody has a definitive answer about why it's something we'd even start doing to begin with.

There are some obvious reasons as to why we like to kiss, but it's important to note that some cultures, particularly more 'primitive' ones, find the practice strange and in some cases, downright unpleasant. We can therefore assume that kissing isn't something ingrained in human behaviour; it's very much a social construct and varies between different cultures.

Here are some of the explanations I've discovered from my research into the practice of kissing:

- **Data collection**
  Your face and mouth are full of sensory information and I'm not just talking about taste buds. Our mouths carry all sorts of data about our health and hygiene. During the act of kissing, we share genetic and immunological information and measure up our potential partners on a deeply biological level. How ... sexy?

- **Psychological signalling**
  Kissing does add the extra senses of taste and smell that contribute to physical intimacy. Not only does it increase closeness, but it establishes openness and trust. It's a physical signal saying, 'I really, really like you, let's do this.' (Alternatively, it can hint at quite the opposite; ignore this at the peril of your own happiness!)

- **Preserving the relationship**
  The kiss is an expression of intimacy and a means of sustaining and enhancing feelings.

- **Seduction**
  It would be fairly obvious to say that the more penetrative tongue kiss simulates potential activity down the track and... you get the idea.

It releases a whole heap of chemicals related to making us feel good and encouraging bonding. Kissing has much the same effect as hugs, releasing such love drugs as oxytocin and producing the same reactions.

Unite Through Food

Food, glorious food! Create beautiful rituals through one of the wonderful necessities of life. We eat throughout our marriage and relationships and well, every part of our lives. From my time as a marriage counsellor, however, I'm not convinced that Australian culture uses this shared experience to strengthen our relationships like, say the Italians? You may well have planned exciting and romantic dates in the early days at your favourite restaurants or on the beach and gazed hopefully and lovingly into each other's eyes. What about the everyday upkeep of our relationships?

> Some of the best conversations you'll ever have will be over a meal.

Some of the best conversations you'll ever have will be over a meal. It's universally acknowledged as a great time to discuss a variety of topics, even difficult ones. Don't underestimate the psychological and emotional benefits of a meal together, namely social connection, intellectual stimulation, relaxation and romance.

Use some of these strategies for curating culinary cohesion as a couple:

Give up multi-tasking

Hands up who eats in front of the TV or accompanied by a screen? Thought so. The trap of living with an unnecessary sense of urgency to be entertained, to work and of course to be ever-present on social media can put you in a state of chronic toxic stress and make you sick, including terrible indigestion! Turn off the screens and allow meals to be the perfect time to talk about your highs and lows. It will also slow you down and you will likely eat less.

> It's all wonderful to decide to 'eat together more often,' but why not handwrite a specific goal such as 'Eat together as a family at the table three times per week on these days...'?

Invest the time in home cooking

Savouring the satisfaction of creating a dish and likewise having your partner prepare something for you is something you can both put loving care and effort into. (Hello husband, I hope you're reading.) Sure, it's still a meal, but when it's made with love, it's super special and tastes oh so much better! It's like a tiny, tasty gift at the end of a long day.

Can't cook? Try learning

This is the perfect joint activity. There are awesome options to do a cooking class, or learn about local food or culinary tradition in just about any town or city. Putting in the effort to improve yourself for the sake of your relationship shows a great deal of love and dedication, and it'll taste good too.

Create the mood

Arty and bright or warm and dark tonight? Use those funky little string lights, draw something, use aromatic candles and swoon to the music. Want to feel sophisticated? Throw on some classical music. Tweak the atmosphere in your house and bang—date night is on.

Relax and enjoy yourselves!

Just because you switched off technology doesn't mean you need to be super formal. Sit back, relax and chill. Why not kick back on the floor whilst eating for a change? If there are little munchkins in the house, they'll love a snackable spread on a blanket. Plenty of other cultures do it.

Make it habitual

It's all wonderful to decide to 'eat together more often,' but why not handwrite a specific goal such as 'Eat together as a family at the table three times per week on these days...'? Put this up on the fridge for ALL to see and practice, practice, practice. Keep each other accountable and after 30 days, it'll be the start of a norm of uniting through food for you!

No More Phubbing

Not fibbing or blubbering. I'm talking phubbing! Phone + Snubbing. This is a behaviour I've sadly discovered; one I am still guilty of and I'm guessing you could well be too. It's certainly a phenomenon in the counselling room and has a much greater impact on relationships than we realise.

Not a week goes by when cyber-related challenges aren't raised in the counselling room.

In my experience, the most common areas for concern that are brought up in counselling are:

- Frequent late-night use of the internet
- Addictive games and related conversations with people unknown to partners
- Obsessive protection of phones that never leave their side
- Lack of attention to the excessive hours children spend online, sometimes resulting in aggression or moodiness

The fact that technology is advancing at lightning speed and the enormous impact it has on the way we do things is nothing new. I can't wait to download the latest app for fear of missing out! Last week it was for sleep monitoring and this week it's a new funky navigational one. Social media networks have become the main channels of communication for so many of us—you must have been living in a cave if you haven't heard of or used Facebook, Messenger, SnapChat, Twitter, YouTube, Flickr, Instagram, WhatsApp and Tinder. This is where friction with your loved ones begin. Regular prioritisation of your phone—to check the weather, find package-free wholefoods to engineer that delectable dish or to check the footy scores—over your love for your partner, results in 'phubbing'.

I'm the first one to admit to being amused or mesmerised for way too long by a certain hand-held device portraying enviable, captivating pictures, data or ideas whilst my own family was seeking my attention. I've phubbed them often and am ashamed of it. This shocking behavioural phenomenon is a real word and a real 'thing'. By engaging in this dreadful 'technoference' I am depriving those most important to me of the emotional attention they deserve. Furthermore, it can make us feel downright miserable.

Neuroscience News reported the findings of a team of psychologists at Ruhr-Universität Bochum (RUB) led by Dr Phillip Ozimek:[39]

Private and professional social networks can promote higher levels of depression if users mainly use them passively, compare themselves with others socially and these comparisons harm self-esteem.

> Marriages and children flourish when they are not constantly receiving the message that your phone is more important than them.

'It is important that this impression that everyone else is better off, can be an absolute fallacy,' says the psychologist. 'In fact, very few people post on social media about negative experiences. However, the fact that we are flooded with these positive experiences on the Internet gives us a completely different impression.'

Correspondingly, the Relationships Australia Indicator survey cited that a concerning and significant proportion (around 50%) of both men and women indicated that there had been a negative effect on their relationship due to a current or former partner spending too much time on the internet instead of with them or their family.[40] This is so sad! Marriages and children flourish when they are not constantly receiving the message that your phone is more important than them. The happiest head start to your child's life is a secure 'attachment'. That is, they need to know they can count on you when they need to, that you love them and you need them. It also means joining them in response to their 'bids' for your attention. The frequency of requests such as, 'Watch me balance this fidget spinner on my nose, Dad' can be annoying, however from what I hear from the wise elderly, they'll be grown up and gone way too soon. Watch the fidget spinner now: turn toward your children, your family and your partner.

> Do we have a no-screen zone in our house or time frames when we converse real-time in the flesh?

Here are some practical questions to ask each other:

- What do we perceive is a reasonable amount of screen time per day?
- Can we incorporate a fun challenge with an incentive to reduce it? (Many devices have a built-in time tracker to keep you informed)
- Do we set a good example for screen usage etiquette for children? (That is, putting down your screen, engaging with emotional attentiveness and eye contact or keeping them away from the dinner table.)
- Do we share new apps related to our interests or games apps?
- What apps, websites, podcasts or blogs can we both use to enrich our relationship? A great example is the 'Gottman Card Decks' app for couples.
- Do we feel comfortable leaving our phone unattended and face up for our partner to view?
- Are we comfortable to be online friends with ex-partners, old school friends or new acquaintances of the opposite sex?
- Who do we agree is acceptable for us to chat online with?

- Have we ever gifted money to a cause, a person or organisation and not told each other?
- Do we have a no-screen zone in our house or time frames when we converse real-time in the flesh?
- Do we agree with what each other posts on social media sites?

My relationship therapy often incorporates the process of couples creating their own customised rules to prevent social media infiltrating their relationships and then using this set of rules to enhance their connection. The first step is awareness, so be proactive and discuss any concerns with your partner. Here are some specific ideas that I've collaborated on with couples and found effective:

- Redirect work phone calls to a colleague or subordinate on specified days or evenings.
- Prohibit screen time past 8 pm (put them in a technology box at the front door).
- Delete the offending app from your smartphone for a set time to disrupt unhealthy patterns. Replace it with one that encourages a new activity together such as fitness goals.
- Incorporate the use of technology for private romantic gestures or methods for gratitude. Share your latest app find with your partner so they're always included.
- Mention your partner in some of your online posts so they know you're proud of them. If you're in a relationship, why would your online world reflect anything different?
- Buy an old-style alarm clock and keep phones out of the bedroom.
- Plan device-free outings. Imagine that! You'll have to re-

member it as you won't even be able to take a photo.

- Have a technology detox regularly, such as every Sunday.

If you have small children, create a caring legacy by modelling behaviour and respect for others—the kind you hope to see imitated, especially when they are teenagers! As much as social media is an effective tool in connecting relationships, it can also lead to their demise. Stop phubbing, be still, be present and you give and get the gift of NOW. There are some great online safety quizzes to check their understanding about sharing their images, giving out their information and what to do about online bullying. It could save their life.

I love that we've become even more connected thanks to technology. Long-distance relationships are enhanced by it and those living or travelling abroad feel closer than ever to their family and friends they've left behind. In day-to-day life however, screens are often an unwanted third person in the relationship. When both partners are screen-addicted, it's some sort of crazy foursome where the only real connection is the charging port that sustains this unhealthy attachment.

Enjoy the wonders of technology to be entertained, organised and informed, but if you're withholding information from your partner about your screen use, then that could be your red flag.

TAKEAWAY TOOLS

Maintaining a loving and supportive relationship is one of the best parts of being committed to someone for life. Ensuring that you are regularly engaging with your partner in an activity that allows you to have fun together is a wonderfully necessary part of nurturing your relationship to ensure its longevity.

- First, find out what your relationship status is: flatmates who share a bed or frenemies who butt heads over who left the milk out? Start focusing on what your relationship might need, to flourish from there.
- Accept the package deal of friends and family that come with your commitment to your partner, integrate healthy boundaries and learn to respect them.
- Get over the cliché: date nights are fun and effective in reigniting an ember into a burning flame.
- Start talking about things other than the weather or your children's schedules. Open up to communication on anything and everything.
- Accept compliments from your partner and start dishing them out too. Start small and work your way up to meaningful, eye holding 'I love you's.'

- Practice intimacy—it is good for you and that's a scientific fact. You have a feel-good factory standing right next to you, so start with a hug and end with a kiss for better health.
- Nourish yourself and your partner with the magic of food and all the rituals associated with it.
- Put down your phone. STOP PHUBBING the ones you love, and they will love you more.

PARENTING

Consistent with our relational nature of creation, our inherent sense of altruism is what does bring happiness from parenting. Besides, who wouldn't source joy from your 'mini-me's' that replicate all your good and bad habits?

Parenthood and Happiness?

Esther and Phil's eyes shone from across the counselling room as they reminisced about their wildly exciting lifestyle in New York. They had both flourished in their highly paid jobs, revelled in their common interest as 'foodies' and partied hard with an interesting and eclectic group of friends that envied their loving relationship. They'd married ten years before I met them and now, I listened empathetically to their subsequent gruelling experience of the IVF roller coaster for the ensuing five years in their desperate attempt to have children.

They'd moved back to Australia for further family support with a dream that their parents could enjoy a grandchild. Throughout this relocation, they continued to enjoy a loving marriage as they united during the IVF process with the hopeful vision of their own family.

As the years passed, Esther's 39-year-old biological clock ticked mercilessly and they grew impatient and sad. They suffered the indescribable pain from constant miscarriage disappointments, and grief at their failed expectations of what they'd assumed would be the natural next step in their union. Hope was fading rapidly. Their emptiness was overwhelming as friends in their circle began the next exciting phase of sending their children to school.

Thanks to modern medicine, the cause was pinpointed and Esther prepared to become even more of a 'pincushion' for the fertility procedures ahead. Lovemaking by now was a chore. It was scheduled and lacklustre. With delight, however, Esther became pregnant and young Dylan arrived 15 weeks early with many of the usual pre-term complications that come with an early birth. At the time of our therapy he was 18 months old and the light of their world; however, they were still attending frequent medical appointments for impending heart surgery. Their relationship by that stage was sexless and often hostile.

When I questioned them on the usual, 'When was the last phase in your life when your relationship felt connected and loving?' They replied, 'Before Dylan was born'. Understandable.

For all the projects we undertake in life, there's one task we just can't afford to get wrong: parenting! Does parenting provide happiness? In one word—no! This sentiment seems to echo even amongst the fortunate parents who sail through reproduction with minimal health challenges.

This idea is consistently repeated in social science literature. However, I have come to this conclusion: consistent with our relational nature of creation, our inherent sense of altruism is what does bring happiness from parenting. Besides, who wouldn't source joy from your 'mini-me's' that replicate all your good and bad habits?

Sociologist Jennifer Glass and her colleagues researched 22 countries and revealed that there are two different narratives when it comes to examining the effects of children on the happiness of mid-life parents. 'The first concerns having minor children at home, which results almost uniformly in less happiness. Both men and women report less personal happiness and less happy marriages when there are minor children around the house. Kids are often noisy and disruptive, and they seem to take an especially large toll on older parents. What about the effects on happiness of just having children? Here, the effects are gendered: mothers experience less happiness than childless women do, but fatherhood now makes men happier. That didn't use to be the case…but it has changed as dads have become more involved with childrearing over the past 45 years.'[41] As women soar toward busting the 'glass ceiling', it makes sense that they now achieve greater fulfilment from contributing to their work, community and other independent pursuits. Again, this is where the Baby Boomers and Generation X'ers—as the trailblazers for having both partners working in paid employment—could well be ill-equipped for remaining aligned. Unless you're continually checking in with who is expected to do what, it is little wonder that resentment sets in when everyone in the household arrives home at 7pm and there's no roast on the table nor clean, pressed clothes for tomorrow.

In his analysis of Glass' findings, Nicholas H Wolfinger notes that the blunt psychometric instruments offered in their studies may not encompass what children do have to offer! I know many of us will graciously proclaim the inherent benefits and bliss derived from wiping dirty noses and bottoms of the small beings that quaintly resemble ourselves. However, the beautiful gift of giving and nurturing is what I believe is true joy.

Parenting means so much—the sheer weight of this role certainly overwhelms me at times. The impact of a mother can map the route to happiness or otherwise. Of course, in many situations, the absence of a mother can lead children to forge incredible bonds with fathers or other significant carers. However, of all the relationships we form throughout our lives, the relationship between a mother and child is one of the most important. Some mothers have little concept of their significance and some worry too much.

What fascinates me is how much that relationship can develop and change over our lives. Our base wellbeing is provided by a feeling of safety from a healthy attachment early in our lives and depends on the patterns of interaction with our parents.

When mother and infant enjoy satisfying connectedness such as during breastfeeding and with eye and skin contact, they are rewarded with oxytocin and dopamine. As parents respond to and anticipate the baby's needs in their first two years of life, the baby's neurons are connecting. Our early attachment experiences shape this process.

It's a bit like the formwork that supports and protects a concrete construction until it is strong enough to stand independently and weather the elements in years to come. That is, we lay down the structures for us to healthily 'self-regulate' our responses in the future.[42] As highlighted by neuroscientist Dr Sarah McKay, even the mother's brain is reshaped through a mix of pregnancy-related hormones and the intense sensory and emotional stimulation provided by her newborn.[43] The product of that stable attachment includes a healthy regulation of the heart and being in tune with your own bodily functions, being attuned to others through empathy, managing fear as well as analysing risks and managing impulses. Massive isn't it!

In summary, when the child has this early safe connection, they're more likely to approach a wonderful life and its challenges versus avoiding it. A happy well-adjusted child translates to a less stressful marriage! On a side note, Dr McKay's extensive research unveiled that 'baby brain' is not a real thing and you could well be smarter for it! Maybe looking for your phone whilst holding it can be blamed on sleep deprivation though?

I've counselled many parents confronted by their gender-role ideology. Women in particular feel the pressure of having to be inherently interested in and good at parenting simply because of their gender. Maybe you're hoping to be a parent, missing yours or longing for an improved parent-child relationship?

I successfully worked with Esther and Phil for over two years as they reinvented their relationship as parents. Successful strategies were found for these areas of focus:

- The root cause of Esther's inability to assertively ask for help when pushed beyond her parenting limits (mostly due to lack of sleep).
- Grief around the inability to meet idyllic (and unrealistic!) perceptions of motherhood and fatherhood.
- Family cultural differences around expectations of roles and responsibilities.
- Boundaries around sacred time alone and together as a couple.
- Restoring passion and fulfilling sexual intimacy.

The Lifecycle of a Parent

It's no wonder new mothers experience varying levels of anxiety: their new child is totally and completely dependent on them for its survival. The parental impact (particularly the mother's) on her child's brain is extensive and profound. She couldn't be more influential during childhood stages. Interestingly, this influence decreases as the child reaches adolescence and adulthood. It's quite a role reversal as mothers can become less prominent and more reliant on their child for advice and support (technological support comes to mind!). As health declines, parents can become dependent on the child for both mental and physical survival. You could say, what goes around comes around and there is no more relevant example of this than in the cycle of a parent:

> More couples than not experience a significant decline in relationship happiness following the birth of their first child that doesn't seem to be consistent with what they deem is supposed to be the happiest time in their life.

Infancy: As mentioned, our sense of safety and well-being from a healthy attachment depends on the patterns of interaction with our parents, which begins in infancy. When a child experiences this safe connection, they're more likely to approach a wonderful life with its challenges versus avoiding it. More couples than not experience a significant decline in relationship happiness following the birth of their first child that doesn't seem to be consistent with what they deem is supposed to be the happiest time in their life. It makes sense even for those who don't suffer from postnatal depression to experience a decrease in couple satisfaction as a result of less quality time, less intimacy, less sex and attempting not to act psychotic on one hour's sleep.

Toddlers and preschool: Parents then become nurturers and teachers and guide toddlers toward safe choices. This is particularly important as they become mobile and assertive! Parents help shape their child's behaviour toward socialisation by adopting loving and firm boundaries to support their future resilience and knowledge of consequences. The greatest possible outcome here is a curious child: one that is focused, is able to freely play, is sometimes self-reliant and mostly cheerful. They decrease your hygiene standards, may ruin your sex life but guaranteed to level up your spontaneity.

School age: As the greater environment and peers broaden the psychosocial and cognitive abilities of the child's world, the parent-child relationship continues to remain the most important influence on their development. It's often natural here that the primary carer has greater freedom to work and therefore has to juggle their requirement to provide that responsive, attentive, warm and loving environment and yet still maintain firm boundaries. *Sigh*! Even in the case of significant change such as divorce, the relationship between the parent and child remains a more important positive factor to the child's psychological development than any impact from other possible changes.

Adolescence: Traditionally seen as a time of conflict and crazy chaos, this can equally be a wonderful time when parents can enjoy what Clinical Professor Dr Dan Siegel terms the 'Essence of Adolescence'.[44] This is the emotional spark, social engagement, novelty-seeking and creative exploration stage. I notice that when there are both positive male and female parental influences here, teens fare best. For parents who have no contact with the other biological parent, this can take the form of a grandparent,

> Maybe the worn down, anxious, fearful and exhausted 'I can't do this' feeling is exactly where your transformation begins when you ask for help?

uncle, aunt or respected friend. This is also an interesting stage for parents as they can be transitioning to mid-life around this time! We can see how in the previous stages, the significance of maintaining that secure attachment is so imperative. I notice that couples face similar stress to that of the early years in navigating their roles to provide a united front for boundary setting as their teen prepares for the big, wide world. Sleep deprivation may be revisited whilst out collecting your new party-goer in the wee hours or simply lying awake worrying about them returning home on their probationary licence. One particular pitfall to avoid where multiple children are involved is that often parents are not equally respected and children sometimes take sides based on their personality types. An example is this war analogy where mother and son sit in Germany, the father and daughter in France and the youngest daughter in Switzerland as the peacemaker! I have some great discussion points on this later in the chapter.

Toolbox Topic Six: Parenting

Adults: Many adults have an active relationship with their parents and now relate to each other as equals. Some parents remain authoritarian but inevitably come to rely on their children as they become physically weaker. This can bring both stress and fulfilment as parents and adult children redefine their relationship. Men are traditionally seen as less communicative, more independent and less social. This means there is potential for some men to become even more so as their testosterone levels or health declines. I've heard of many traditional family situations in recent generations where the meek and mild wife eventually takes on the matriarchal role as the couple age. It seems quite evident that parents today are closer to their adult children than in previous generations. We are enjoying a trend where we can enjoy a more intimate relationship that is closer and more equal than ever existed in the past.

I wonder if the challenges throughout any of these stages correspond to growth in our role as parents when we reach out to others? Maybe the worn down, anxious, fearful and exhausted 'I can't do this' feeling is exactly where your transformation begins when you ask for help? In honour and respect of all imperfect parents in all forms, I need to let you know that I'm sure you've contributed to greatness you might never realise and that you deserve love and self-compassion. Most of all, give your partner all the recognition they deserve for their best attempts to cope with your little darlings.

Parental Self-Compassion

Have words to the effect of, 'I never signed up for this!' ever leaked out of your mouth? Maybe it was whilst desperately wrangling a fierce-looking child as you wrenched them away from their screaming sibling? Was is it in the form of a frustrated sigh whilst on all fours trying to wipe up the aftermath of an upturned bowl of cooked rice now stuck to the furniture? Maybe you'd contemplated this during the dark hours nursing a feverish baby and wracked by worry as you calculated the precious hours of sleep that you might never get back? Could it have been the nervous anticipation as you waited up for the newly licensed driver to return home safely?

> It's an exciting ripple effect when we can mentor generations that promote dynamic and flourishing relationships and families. It's life-changing and certainly rocks my world.

Run into another parent down the street and the majority of them will usually mention how 'busy' they are. Most of us want to provide a life that was just as good as, or better than, what we had.

Many mums and dads are feverishly seeking to keep up with the abundance of activities on offer that expose our children to a myriad of pre- or after-school sports and arts in the hope they'll be the best that they can be. In the meantime, we can neglect what's inherently important—the relationship we have with them and the example we set.

I love to think of the impact of the amazing people I work with in counselling on their future generations—with their newly acquired conflict resolution and communication skills amongst other things. Yes! It's an exciting ripple effect when we can mentor generations that promote dynamic and flourishing relationships and families. It's life-changing and certainly rocks my world. Similar to the earlier Toolbox Topic of aiming for the best version of yourself, this concept is just as important: whilst rearing your children, ensure that your relationship is a solidly, renovated safehouse that you will lovingly maintain as you nurture your kids.

Whether you've mucked up at work, forgotten the dress-up day at school or your teenager refuses to detach from that online game, your brain is the key to responding positively to all these challenges. We won't always seamlessly execute the greatest response, but when we do there's certainly no point in continuing to repeat that pattern of overwhelm. The secret is to learn skills to manage anxiety and frustration.

I draw your attention to the importance of nurturing parental physical and psychological wellbeing. It's our responsibility to model this for our children by focusing on our continued growth and change. Whilst parenting involves plenty of self-sacrifices, we create a beautiful nurturing environment for our children when we nourish ourselves. Here are three examples:

Sweat so you don't forget: You'll recall how to rejuvenate your mind in Toolbox Tip Two. This is a reminder to boost it with exercise. Sorry mum and dad bods, there's no avoiding this one. Your brain loves it and you've got a better chance of keeping up with your children's energy levels too. Encourage your little student cherubs to take short bursts of exercise before they try to accomplish a new task as they'll have a far better chance of remembering how to do it. Meanwhile you'll be able to focus better at work, and improve your comprehension both for tasks at hand and up to 48 hours later! Don't set yourself up for failure. Start slow and build up to longer stints of exercise so it's a habit. Repetition and consistency are key. The benefits will undoubtedly flow through to all your relationships when you're feeling better within yourself from all those happy endorphin chemicals, as well as looking great.

> A parent with a rich private life that features integrity through contribution as well as plenty of fun launches healthy, balanced children to their success!

A beautiful mind: Parenting involves so many joyful, exciting, sad and frustrating twists and turns. For this reason, it's handy to develop a game plan for being more flexible and resilient and able to deal with challenges in the most optimum way. As a start, perhaps you could set aside some regular 15-minute time slots to visualise, plan and write down what your best version of you looks like? Your core values about parenting and relationships can be quite different from the next person. Who is the ideal you as a parent, sibling, daughter, son etc? What blockages exist that are stopping you from making any changes required? You *can* do anything you put your mind to and inspiring your children should be right up there in your top priorities. Seek out authors or experts in the fields you're challenged by and enjoy a beautiful mind.

Stay social: A parent with a rich private life that features integrity through contribution as well as plenty of fun launches healthy, balanced children to their success!

Here are my top tips for nurturing the social parent:

- **Banish the guilt!** It's not selfish to seek time out, it's healthy. A bolstered social life is not only incredibly fun, but inevitably provides a source of support.
- **Take time out** with your tribe! Not always, but us mums often have way more words than our partners can handle. Save some for your gal-pals at regular catch-ups. Whilst they won't often seek it out, most dads sure appreciate man time. Engineering those golf days, surfing, mixing beer in those trendy breweries or whatever it is that makes a dad happy facilitates a fulfilled and relaxed parent.
- **Model great relationships** with your friends, your children's friends, other parents, teachers and family. Those amazing little brains you've created are watching and often mimicking your every move. If we can show them how kind friends behave and how to show respect for others with our language and actions, there's a great chance they'll surprise you with beautiful manners, generosity and love for the people in their community.
- **Nurture your friendships** with returned calls, messages or random acts of kindness. Undoubtedly, the majority of parents are run off their feet. Think what could happen, though, if we all looked a little more outward. How satisfying would it be to brighten a friend's day with a quirky sweet gesture, or

an 'Are you okay?' phone call. Physical distancing through-out the 2020 pandemic certainly put the spotlight on the importance of caring for others in this way.

- **Participate in community events** and work on at least one area of your life where you can give service to benefit others. Consider volunteering as a family and appreciate the united and incredible joy of giving your time for free for a worthy cause.

- **Online groups** unite parents in magnificent ways. It's awe-some to notice open communication when a bunch of parents pull together to contribute when someone faces unexpected illness or strife.

Whether you join some sort of meet-up group, find a new hobby, join a fitness group or chat online, your children

> Many of us fail to see the inherent symptoms of being an imperfect human such as being moody, tired and forgetful.

will benefit from learning about your enriched social life.

Romance and Parenthood in the Same Sentence?

Do you struggle to find the balance between your role as a parent and then as a spouse? You have plenty of company there as everyone finds this a challenge at some point in time. They may well be the two most important and rewarding roles of your life, but juggling both can be most difficult.

You *can* achieve balance and the romance that comes with it! Try my ten tips, designed to help you think, feel and act differently to get you on your way to a happier partner, happier children and most importantly, a happier you!:

1. Think of yourself as human

Many of us fail to see the inherent symptoms of being an imperfect human such as being moody, tired and forgetful. Whilst excelling at things feels fabulous, recognising your limitations and embracing them is another thing! Why not lose your aspirations for 'Supermum' or 'Wonderdad' sometimes? A newborn is sure to take the focus off your spouse during this tricky time. However, recognising each other's lack of resilience in the face of severe lack of sleep will certainly be appreciated!

2. Discover your definitions

What is your definition of a 'Prizewinning Partner', 'Stepford Wife', or 'The Perfect Husband?' How do you describe a 'loving parent?' Where did these ideas come from—a movie? Are you aiming to recreate what your parents did, or do you plan to do everything differently? It's worth considering, as operating inconsistently with your values and trying to meet unhealthy expectations of yourself can leave you feeling like a 'bad' or 'absent' parent or partner.

3. Look at the big picture

In the grand scheme of things, your kids will not likely remember you forgot the money for the school bake sale (I forgot again this year!). Your partner will probably not remember you were ten minutes late last week. They *will* remember the things that matter. Make it non-negotiable to get to that important footy game or ballet concert they are super excited about. Take a moment to send him or her some words of encouragement for their big presentation this week. Focus on what counts. I love the 'Ten Rule' that the iconic Oprah

> Healthy boundaries involve consistent child bedtimes, healthy routines and self-compassion.

Winfrey outlined on one of her TV episodes. 'Will this matter be important in 10 minutes, 10 hours, 10 days, 10 months or 10 years?' It sure helps me put things in perspective.

4. Minimise the guilt

Carrying the heavy sack of 'the times when you couldn't be there' guilt, or a 'Clark Griswold' (National Lampoon's Vacation epic movie parenting failure) gets in the way of being the best parent and partner that you can be today. Do yourself and everyone a favour and forgive yourself. It's a choice to forgive so learn from it and launch yourself to success as a result.

5. Let go of worry

Similarly, worry stands in our way of being our best selves. If worry tricks you into thinking you're doing something useful, remember that it's actually usually pointless. The next time you find yourself ruminating about upsetting someone or forgetting something, either *do* something about it (e.g. ask them how they feel) or simply let it go and focus on moving forward.

6. Maintain healthy boundaries

A lack of boundaries leads to children constantly interrupting, insufficient private time and taking on too much. Healthy boundaries involve consistent child bedtimes, healthy routines and self-compassion. Do you have a regular 'date' with your partner to protect your relationship? Do you intentionally provide consistent emotional attentiveness for your children so that it facilitates time for your romantic relationship too?

7. Focus on teamwork

You and your partner must be a united front. This means agreeing about what kind of parents and partners you want to be and constantly supporting each other. Hold regular discipline discussions in private then remember to back your partner in the parenting decisions. Show appreciation for each other's efforts. Parenting is relentless, so simple words can go a long way!

8. Model healthy behaviours

You are mentoring your children every day. Show your children the value of having life balance and prioritising relationships by modelling this in your actions. The children benefit from seeing you put your relationship with your spouse first at times. Date night booked?

9. Communicate with everyone… including yourself!

Never forget the value of open, honest communication. Firstly, regularly tap into your feelings and needs, then be brave enough to seek feedback from your partner and children. Don't assume they know what's in your head. Healthy communication leads to more balance and harmony for everyone!

10. Romance and intimacy is paramount

Remember your first date? Why not recreate those early days with something reminiscent? Can you improve on it with a wonderful surprise? Reach out to friends or family to help facilitate time out with regular babysitting. Be okay to ask for help as parenting and partnering isn't always easy.

Fly in Fly Out Parenting

A sizeable proportion of my counselling practice includes couples where one partner commutes interstate or overseas. Whilst there are so many upsides to this work, here are some of the common challenges I hear:

- Relationships become strained and one parent often takes on the role of single parent.
- Children are impacted emotionally spending time looking forward to Mum or Dad's return and then having to say goodbye again.
- FIFO workers may find it difficult to adjust from single life to family life.
- Both partners need downtime, time with each other and time with their children.
- A sense of isolation and loneliness that can lead to depression.

- Fatigue due to very long shifts (for the parent at home and the person away).
- Missing significant events such as birthdays and weddings.
- Often high levels of stress.
- Struggling to feel part of the community due to long stretches away.
- A sense of not 'belonging' anymore.

Thankfully we have the benefit of technology to keep working partners in touch with their families. It certainly doesn't replace touch, but a quick handheld 'FaceTime' at the soccer match is a wonderful tool. Other ideas to foster greater connection are:

- Plan ahead with class teachers to invite the working parent in for a 'Show and Share' about their job. You can engineer any job to sound exciting!
- Exchange drawings or notes in lunch boxes.
- Plan regular one-on-one breakfast dates for each child with the working parent before school, particularly if you have multiple children.
- Arrange for a spontaneous school pick-up by the working partner. It might be infrequent, but avoid being too rigid in your roles as these surprises will be memorable.
- Create a special regular ritual such as 'Saturday morning pancake cook-up' when the working parent is home that creates a special connection.
- Create an online shared photo album or scrapbook of events to share important achievements such as awards or exciting things to share with the working parent.

- Draw up a special calendar featuring input from the children on days when a travelling parent arrives home.
- Make your own private YouTube channel with a home 'news report' made by the children and one by the absent parent.
- Importantly, ensure both parents are understanding of hectic times during their schedules such as meetings and evening bath/mealtimes!

It's helpful for parents to collaborate on an 'insurance plan' for how you'll transition again each time you reunite. This can include asking yourselves:

- What down-time does each partner require when they return home to rejuvenate from long working hours or long days spent with the children?
- What roles and responsibilities at home can be clearly outlined and allocated to relieve resentment?
- What are you looking forward to as a couple/family?
- How are you maximising financial rewards? Do you need a goal to conclude commuting within a certain timeframe?

This lifestyle can certainly provide amazing benefits such as greater financial rewards, relief from the standard working hours and for some, thousands of frequent flyer points! With planning and effort, many commuting parents enjoy a fun and connected relationship with their family.

A United Front

Ever found yourself aghast at your partner's consequences of a mere 'Stop that' for your child's clothes left on the floor for the umpteenth time? Were you shocked when they admonished your teen with no Wi-Fi access for two weeks when they didn't meet curfew for the first time? If you're a parent, and likely tackling this role with the other person who made them, you've probably disagreed with how they approached discipline at some point.

> It's important to maintain a feeling of safety and security by keeping that fishing, skating or movie date you promised your child. Equally, you need to follow through with a promised negative consequence.

To ensure you are both presenting a united front to your children, it is helpful to discuss these questions with your partner:

- Do you appreciate how you were disciplined?
- If anything, what would you change about your childhood?
- How close did you feel to your family and if not, why not?
- Do you remember how bed and mealtimes were handled?
- What were the consequences for poor choices when you were a child?
- Do you desire to mirror your parents' methods?
- How are your respective answers to the above similar or different?

Whilst you cannot anticipate every scenario, I encourage couples to conduct regular behind-the-scenes discussions to determine your disciplinary style. It is natural to discover you have inconsistent approaches. Importantly, back each other in front of the children then discuss it later. Your children will be quick to work around the more flexible parent.

Another crucial aspect is promise-keeping. It's important to maintain a feeling of safety and security by keeping that fishing, skating or movie date you promised your child. Equally, you need to follow through with a promised negative consequence.

Understandably, parents become worn down by the repetition required to reinforce appropriate boundaries. Un-

When coupled with a warm and loving environment, children enjoy the security of understanding firm boundaries as they grow into confident people who respect their parents and others. You will have equipped them to self-regulate their responses to challenges and failures as well as have the responsibility to be self-disciplined contributors to society.

fortunately, when you don't follow through with that consequence you've warned them about, children fail to learn the natural effect of poor behaviour. Shielding them from the slightest discomfort now ensures they miss out on powerful lessons for handling frustration and disappointment later in life. Consequences can be positive reinforcement or negative to discourage. They need to be immediate and consistent.

When coupled with a warm and loving environment, children enjoy the security of understanding firm boundaries as they grow into confident people who respect their parents and others. You will have equipped them to self-regulate their responses to challenges and failures as well as have the responsibility to be self-disciplined contributors to society.

Yes, parents, it's relentless, thankless and often heart-wrenching to see your child miss out on what they enjoy sometimes—but worth it. They might even thank you in a few decades when they have children!

Parenting in the Fast Lane

How's your schedule? Can you spontaneously fit in a drink and a play with the neighbours or do they need to wait three weeks? Do you allow time in your weekday either to be with the children after school or for yourself with nil commitments? I mean, nothing else to do, at all.

Do you worry your children won't be the best versions of themselves if they're not involved in all the wonderful activities on offer? What if they miss out on finding their true gift? What if their friends learn new skills that yours don't? What if…?

Here, I'm talking about too much, too often, too soon and often all at the same time.

Not only does it have a detrimental impact on your well-being, but also that of the children. It certainly is nothing to be proud of. In a world that often lauds a hectic, action-packed lifestyle, it's important to remember that busyness should not be a badge of honour.

Overloading and pushing ourselves and our children to the limit is harmful. Did you know that there's a noticeable shift in our generation of children who are gradually moving away from an internal towards an external locus of control? That is, they're focussing more on external methods to find happiness instead of looking within. They're so overstimulated, entertained and surrounded by toys, they're losing the ability to self-regulate, self-soothe and find contentment for themselves. Frightening! No wonder there is a rise in anxiety, depression and narcissism.

Parents are falling into the trap of 'Milkshake Multitasking,' as neuroscientist Dr Caroline Leaf calls it.[45] She says we can shift between different tasks in rapid succession, but it's impossible to truly multitask. This rapid switching results in neurochemical chaos and brain damage. As we're frantically switching between those emails to pay the footy and dance fees, checking Instagram and listening to our child read, there's nothing of quality occurring and we're easily confused and exhausted.

> I don't want a medallion of muddled madness, but a cordon of courage. It will signify that we bravely didn't scribble chaos in our blank margins of life and that encouraged the children to harness their inner resourcefulness to face life's challenges resulting in their innovation and success.

The way to remedy this is to allow 'margin'. It's my favourite word and denotes the space on the side of your page. It is the spare room for attentive conversations, playing on the floor, drawing with chalk on the driveway, following a butterfly and running bare feet outside. I was one of the lucky ticket holders of a home bike stunt show recently. It was complete with hand-drawn tickets, promotional signs and obstacles. Priceless! Margin can be the column for one-on-one time with a child without guilt or time pressure. It's the allocated distance between your to-do list on the other side of the paper that's lined with endless tasks.

Little Johnny and Janita are more likely to become masters of their destiny if we allow them the breadth to do so. We can certainly nurture their talents, but let's not scrawl over their childhood with busyness in the process!

I don't want a medallion of muddled madness, but a cordon of courage. It will signify that we bravely didn't scribble chaos in our blank margins of life and that encouraged the children to harness their inner resourcefulness to face life's challenges resulting in their innovation and success.

Parenting Through Separation

It would be remiss of me not to consider tips on supporting children through separation and divorce.

Dependent upon their age, children cannot always communicate with words to express possible confusion or grief. Their responses to their parents' separation may be expressed in behaviour. Some children become very withdrawn. They lack knowledge about the importance of discussing the separation changes or missing the absent parent. Younger children may become very 'clingy' for fear of losing their remaining parent. Others may 'regress' in behaviour and toilet training. Some act younger than they did before the separation. Nightmares are not uncommon, as well as rebellious or aggressive reactions to other children or their parents.

Whilst the separating parents are grappling with their own difficult emotions, it's imperative to remember that the children might be reacting with distress and need your special attention. With time and attentiveness, these behavioural problems disappear. If there has been abuse or their reactions persist over a long period, it is best to seek some professional help.

Children are not immune to the effects of the parent's anguish. The resulting toxic atmosphere of arguments can be fuelled by hurt, sadness, possible guilt and perhaps feeling like a failure. As the adults gradually accept the separation, the children are more likely to do the same. Despite the enormous difficulty, there are immense benefits for the family to forgive. I've discussed the importance of forgiveness in that when we don't forgive

> The most important gift you can give your children is to remind yourself that you're both their heroes. The biggest reason not to criticise the other parent in front of your children is to not steal an important aspect of themselves—the person who created them.

and later revisit our memories of the supposed wrongdoing, a fear response is produced in our amygdala (the part of our brain responsible for our emotions). This response causes a release of stress hormones, which increases our heart rate and blood pressure. If we keep holding on to our betrayals and anger this response remains active, putting us at risk of developing both mental and physical stress-related illness. Forgiving is not easy. Just like any other difficult or new task, you need to learn how to do it with repetition and consistency. For the sake of your emotional wellbeing though, as well as that of your children, it's worth doing.

The most important gift you can give your children is to remind yourself that you're both their heroes. The biggest reason not to criticise the other parent in front of your children is to not steal an important aspect of themselves—the person who created them. We underestimate the terrible effect of openly discussing how bad the other parent is. This can create serious disharmony as they navigate relationships as an adult and develop unhealthy attachment styles.

Ensure they feel undoubtedly loved and connected to both partners where possible during the separation. Ensure your children know you both still love them and that this will always be the case. Whilst you might be frequently falling apart on the inside, attempting to create a safe and stable environment is paramount. Keeping to routine as much as possible is helpful. Many grown children of divorced parents reflect that they appreciated being prioritised when living arrangements changed.

Other tips to help minimise stress for your children:

Offer age-appropriate data throughout the process. Consider their personalities, fragilities and fears as you deliver information about upcoming changes. Give the children an honest account of the impending changes without blame. Explain who is moving away, and when and where they will see the other parent.

Explain emotions in that tears of sadness help Mummy or Daddy get better and it won't be forever.

Help them express feelings through joining in at playtime. Be patient with unusual behaviours and give them the space to express their feelings about the other parent, even if those feelings are not the same as yours.

Advise other caregivers such as kindergarten or school so they can help, understand and support them.

Set fun goals and be creative with exciting activities for the children to look forward to.

Talk! Children often react under the atmosphere you create. Don't be tempted to rely on your older children for emotional support. Instead, turn to trusted friends, family or a counsellor. It is not uncommon for me to support an individual or a couple through this process to ensure they remain responsible and loving co-parents. Talk to your ex-partner about communication options such as a diary or online synced calendar for important school events, fees, activities and play dates.

You can make peace for your children knowing that your decision to divorce was considered carefully and over a long period. Realising you gave your marriage 100% to rejuvenate and repair it even without success, you can look back with less regret as you recreate a connected and loving environment for your children.

Step-parenting

According to the Bureau of Statistics, around 47% of divorce in Australia involves those with children and naturally, step-parenting is a huge challenge for many families I work with.[46]

Around one in ten families in Australia are step-families, with at least one child living in the house.

It has been assumed that it was better for children from broken homes to have a step-parent because it offers greater financial stability and another authority figure. Yet it would seem that the possible benefits of introducing a step-parent to the family, such as increased economic and parental resources, might be counteracted by the stress related to establishing a new family structure. Remarriage does not necessarily alleviate the negative effects of growing up with a single parent.

As you'd imagine, there's a plethora of advice about step-parenting, so thought I'd highlight some myths included in the Prepare/Enrich online couple analysis resources I use:[47]

- Our family members will blend well due to our love for each other.
- We will enjoy a better marriage this time.
- Our children will be as excited about our new arrangement as we are.
- The stepchildren will naturally bond with their step-parent over time.

The reality is, it does take time—along with plenty of patience and communication—for children to adjust to a new arrangement. Some will bond quicker than others and some can experience rejection and confusion resulting in resentment. Take time to consider your role as the step-parent and to what extent your influence goes, such as discipline and responsibility for their welfare. It has been noted that the first two years of settling into a blended family can be just as stressful as the first two years following a divorce.

Renovate Your Relationship

The greatest challenge I notice is negative comments being communicated from one biological parent through the children to the other. As difficult as it can be to contain your feelings, I implore separated couples to avoid in all circumstances dragging down a part of their child by criticising their ex-partner in front of them. Your child did not ask for this change in circumstance and their wellbeing is your priority. It is incredibly sad to see children being over-informed before they have the ability to process this information.

Whilst we learn from our previous relationships, we can easily fall back into poor habits such as avoiding conflict or lack of communication. It's not uncommon to be easily triggered and reactive by a similar behaviour with the new partner. It is incredibly important to ensure you can enjoy the benefit of experience with the intention to be a better version of yourself so ensure you've learnt from your own mistakes.

> As difficult as it can be to contain your feelings, I implore separated couples to avoid in all circumstances dragging down a part of their child by criticising their ex-partner in front of them. Your child did not ask for this change in circumstance and their wellbeing is your priority.

I stand in awe of the feedback from well-balanced adults who cherished the love and guidance they received while being raised by a step-parent. Blended families can work when you are adequately prepared for the realities!

Perceptive Parenting Questions

The end of each chapter so far has provided you with some summary tools to consider, but this chapter in particular is one dear to my heart. If you haven't gathered by now, I'm all for communication and asking questions to promote closeness, so instead, here are some thought-provoking questions to support you in your parenting role:

Ask yourself:

- Do I frequently encourage my child? Do I ensure that they know I'm there for them and that I believe in them?
- Do I even communicate that I'm sometimes wrong too?
- Do I ever make allowances for my child to experience discomfort, challenges and disappointments?
- Does my child just obey me or does their behaviour represent a connected relationship that fosters respect?
- Do I secretly want my child to be successful so I will feel auspicious?
- How does my behaviour model qualities that I wish my child to exhibit?
- When I chastise my child, do I ensure my message of love is still communicated at the end?

Ask your young child:

- What is something I often say to you?
- What makes you happy?
- What is my favourite thing to do?
- What makes me sad and what makes you sad?

- How can you tell I love you?
- What am I good at?
- What am I bad at?
- What do you enjoy doing with me?
- What are the five best things about being you?
- How do you show people you care?
- What does it feel like when I hug you?
- If you had three wishes, what would they be?

Ask your older child:
- Who are your three best role models?
- Which five words describe you best?
- Which five words describe me best?
- If you wrote a book, what would it be about?
- How do you describe me to your friends?
- How do you best like helping others?
- What makes you feel thankful?
- How could I do better?
- What makes you feel energised?
- What's a memory that makes you happy?
- What makes you so awesome?
- What makes someone smart?
- What do you long for within your family right now?

I trust you'll enjoy contemplating these questions and maybe even chuckle over some of the answers. Take it one step further and construct a more formal report card for your children to rate you on how you rate on quality time, attentiveness, fair consequences etc.

It's healthy for them to know you're open to feedback and far from perfect!

If you could take just three new strategies prompted by this section, why not jot them down? I encourage you to make them visible at home then diarise in your calendar to check in a month that you're progressing on this often thankless, guilt-ridden, yet unique and incredible role of parenting!

It is never too late to begin, however, the earlier you lay the foundation for warm, loving, but firm boundaries, the greater chance you have of building resilient children and placing less stress on your marriage.

TAKEAWAY TOOLS

The role of a parent changes dramatically as children grow. We go from being solely responsible for the wellbeing of our relationship with our offspring, to being able to offer some guidance, to requiring assistance from our children when we reach our golden years. The only constant throughout this process is that the bond you maintain with your child is fostered in a respectful relationship founded on warm, loving and firm boundaries.

- Parents need to show themselves compassion. You are doing the best you can with what you have, and if you are feeling some areas of 'expertise' are lacking, don't be afraid to seek advice and help.
- Self-care can often be forgotten when you become a parent. Make it a priority as you cannot continue to give if your tank is always running on empty.
- Children have the potential to sabotage the strong connection you have with your partner. Make time for the two of you to keep those romantic flames a burnin'!
- There are unique challenges with fly-in fly-out families; the key here is to value connection in whatever forms you can create it.

- Children need a united front from their parents. Anything less and they quickly learn how to divide and conquer!
- Children are not immune to the effects of their parent's anguish. The resulting toxic atmosphere of arguments can be fuelled by hurt, sadness, possible guilt and feeling a failure. If you are navigating a separation or divorce, ensure the little people in your life are feeling as safe and nurtured as possible.
- Blended families are nothing new, but bear in mind that the first two years of settling into a blended family can be just as stressful as the first two years following a divorce.

Renovate Your Relationship

INFIDELITY

The repercussions of infidelity on not only your current relationship, but many generations to come can include poor physical health, alcohol and substance abuse, post-traumatic stress disorder and even sometimes suicide.

Infidelity is one of the most detrimental and devastating acts a person can commit against their partner. An affair can negatively permeate every single aspect of your original relationship and leave a lasting legacy of distrust and shame for your children in their own relationships.

The Start of a Slippery Path

The repercussions of infidelity on not only your current relationship, but many generations to come can include poor physical health, alcohol and substance abuse, post-traumatic stress disorder and even sometimes suicide.

Many people mistakenly think that infidelity isn't infidelity unless there is sexual contact. The likes of influencers and experts such as Dr Jenny Fitzgerald, Dr Shirley Glass, Dr Sue Johnson, the Relationship Institute Australasia, the Gottman Institute and Esther Perel provide evidence and clarification on what can be defined as infidelity beyond actual physical contact:

He/she dominates your thoughts

You are consumed by thoughts of them when you wake up, when you fall asleep and anytime in between. Most affairs don't start with a steamy sex scene; they start in the mind.

You talk about the difficulties in your current relationship

You may have a few close friends with whom you share your frustrations about your partner, but when you find yourself sharing many of those problems and concerns with this 'special person', you may be crossing the line.

S/he becomes the first person you call

What happens when you get some exciting news, or you've had a dreadful day? Who do you think to call first, him/her or your partner?

Contact outside of 'friendly' hours

If you find yourself communicating at questionable hours, this may be a sign you are engaged in infidelity. Most platonic friends don't text at 2 am.

They 'get' you

When you start to feel like s/he understands you better than your partner, this is a red flag. This usually leads to increased communication with him/her and less communication with your partner: we are more likely to communicate with someone we feel 'gets' us than someone who does not.

You redirect your time

If you find yourself finding excuses or creating more reasons to spend time with him/her, this may be a sign of infidelity. However, this is not limited to just physical time. If you are spending more time texting, emailing, Snapchatting, WhatsApping, Facetiming etc, this may be a sign as well.

You compare your partner to him/her

When talking to your partner, do you think to yourself, *S/he wouldn't respond like this*, or *S/he would be more attentive?* When out with your partner, do you think, *If I were with him/her, I'd be having more fun?* This automatically makes the other person the more favourable one and your partner the second prize winner. Your partner should always be first!

You lie

Lying by omission counts. Leaving out details such as meeting him/her for lunch, deleting messages, or denying any sort of communication with that person at all are all forms of lying. If you must lie, chances are you have something to hide; if you have something to hide, you probably know it's not okay.

There are also a number of myths regarding stereotypical candidates for infidelity, or why people engage in an affair in the first place. Dr Shirley Glass[48] and the Relationship Institute Australasia[49] debunk some of these myths here:

The Soul Mate myth

Attraction to someone else means that your spouse is not the right person. In reality, being attracted to or admiring someone means you're breathing!

Affairs only happen to people with marriage problems

Affairs can occur in happy marriages; in this situation they are more likely the unintentional consequence of attraction, opportunity or failure to follow precautions and honour values.

You can't be friends with people of the opposite sex

Friends of each partner need to be a friend of the marriage.

People who have affairs are not getting enough of what they need

The spouse who gives too little is often more likely to commit adultery, being less invested than the spouse who gives too much.

The Most Common Question: Why?

I've heard lots of admissions as to why partners found themselves involved in physical and/or emotional affairs, with the reasons given varying greatly. Some of these include:

Lack of self-love

Interestingly, offending partners can find themselves in an affair when dissatisfied with themselves. Their new love provides a mirror of fresh adoring eyes which enables them to appreciate what they cannot see in themselves.

Family of origin

In my experience, far too many couples recovering from affairs in my counselling room are the result of previous infidelities in their family of origin (usually parents or grandparents). We can't underestimate the value of the legacy we leave for the next generation.

Lack of nurture

An affair can be an indication of the need to escape from a situation of not being listened to. For women in particular, it is often indicative of a lack of emotional connection and nurture. American self-improvement guru Dale Carnegie summed it up perfectly when he said, 'The sound of a person's name is like music to their ears.' In my opinion, a symphony of two hearts united is performed from the gift of attentiveness.

Starving ego

Some can become addicted to the heightened physical and emotional rush of being with a new person.

Revenge

For mistreatment; when the betrayer finally gives up on the impossible task of trying to please their partner and retaliates by seeking adoration elsewhere.

Lack of intimacy

Intimacy is impacted by the ebb and flow of life's demands and the varying compatibility of a couple's libido (which each partner needs to understand and respect). Despite this, making time for regular sex is paramount in an effective and loving relationship.

> Often, it's the lack of real communication between partners, of expressing your desires, or of being validated or acknowledged that fuels the outburst of crying in the arms of another person.

Lack of investment in yourself and the relationship

Poor attention to keeping fit, healthy and rested can result in a substandard contribution to the relationship, resulting in one partner seeking out validation for their investment elsewhere.

Alcohol and drug use

Partners may escape from possible violence because of their partner's dependency or inability to be fully present with each hangover.

Often, it's the lack of real communication between partners, of expressing your desires, or of being validated or acknowledged that fuels the outburst of crying in the arms of another person.

The Risk of Being Risqué

Many people ask me if pornography is a contributing factor to infidelity and whether it is bad for relationships. This is an extremely controversial topic and always will be. As a relationship therapist, I journey with clients without judgement, respecting their opinions and values. There is quite a lot of data about the use of pornography generally, some of which is alarming. However, studies don't always make the distinction between users being single or in a relationship.

Some interesting statistics from Pornhub, one of the largest pornographic video sharing websites on the internet (but certainly not the only one), give some insight into how pornography is being used by people around the world:[50]

The site attracted a total of 42 billion visitors in 2019 (around 115 million a day). The United States were the biggest users, with Australia in ninth place.

The breakdown of viewing age groups is:
- 18-24: 25 per cent
- 25-34: 36 per cent
- 35-44: 17 per cent
- 45-54: 11 per cent
- 55-64: 7 per cent
- 65-plus: 4 per cent
- Female users increase each year and now make up 32 per cent of worldwide Pornhub traffic.
- The most frequent time for viewing is between 10 pm and 1 am.

- The most popular day is Sunday and the least popular is Friday.
- 76.6% is viewed on a phone, 16.3% on a desktop PC and 7.1% on a tablet.

It's a highly profitable billion-dollar business!

It's impossible to use these statistics as a reason why people commit adultery within their marriage. Pornography is big business and like anything, if indulged in too excessively, is detrimental to your relationship. According to researchers Dr Bryant Paul and Dr Jae Woong Shim in their 2008 study, there were four main reasons why people used pornography:[51]

> It makes sense the greater the discrepancy between partners in attitudes towards porn, the greater the negative impact on the relationship.

Fantasy: Sexual excitement, satisfaction, curiosity, exploration and anonymity

Mood management: Emotional regulation, stress relief and escapism

Habitual use: Habit and convenience

Relationship: Enhancement, skills, novelty

Clinical psychologist Dr Clare Rosoman shows that some of the common outcomes of pornography use for those in a relationship are:[52]

- Feelings of internal conflict such as shame, depression, anxiety and irritability.
- Social withdrawal and guilt over the financial outlay of pornography.
- With frequency, pornography can normalise and desensitise associated behaviours that lead to the pursuit of another person and possible affair. Couples within my counselling room have reported that the partner not involved in the pornography may view it as a betrayal to the relationship. Not only can the partner feel sexually inadequate and threatened by pornography use but find certain new sexual activities objectionable. A new 'sexual script' can be unwelcome.
- Risqué images can start as entertainment, may escalate to compulsions and then distort beliefs and expectations and even become addictions. The user faces difficulty in becoming sexually aroused without pornography. They can lose interest in and engage in fewer sexual experiences with their partner.
- Emotional closeness wanes due to a decrease in trust and pornography can be associated with dishonesty.
- Is there any benefit for relationships? The answer will be very different depending on how the questions are asked and who you ask. For example, people in casual relationships are far less likely to have a problem with pornography than those in long term relationships, who have built a life of trust and support together.

Mutual use of porn has been related to lower levels of distress than when only one partner is using and Dr Debby Herbenick is among those who say that couples using porn together found it easier to discuss sexual wants and fantasies with their partners and had higher relationship satisfaction.[53] Not surprisingly, people who only viewed porn with their partner reported more dedication and higher sexual satisfaction than those who viewed it alone.

It makes sense the greater the discrepancy between partners in attitudes towards porn, the greater the negative impact on the relationship. Most discrepancies involve a male partner using more pornography than the female, which lowers her relationship satisfaction, reduces positive communication, creates instability and more relational aggression and lowers female sexual desire.

In summary, can it lead to affairs? Yes, but not always. Is it good for your relationship? Ask your partner.

Shockwaves From the Tsunami

Only those who trust can find love and happiness. And only those who love can be betrayed. Marriage is a partnership built on love, trust and support, so it follows that recovering from an act of infidelity takes reconciliation, forgiveness and communication from both the betrayer and the betrayed.

> The effect of an affair can be similar to the grief associated with death.

The effect of an affair can be similar to the grief associated with death. It's important to realise that the repercussions of that 'death' affect both partners, including:

198

- Intense emotional deregulation: for the unsuspecting 'injured' partner, any sense of security and safety has been shattered.
- Feelings such as hurt, anger, fear, disgust, sadness, shame and guilt that can be experienced by both partners.
- Symptoms of depression, grief, anxiety and post-traumatic stress disorder.
- Alcohol and other substance abuse.
- Suicide attempts/completion.
- Physical health problems.
- Skewed assumptions, beliefs and sometimes permanent change in their perceived meaning of life. For example, 'I thought I could trust you. Now, I don't trust you anymore and I don't trust anybody else either.'
- Injured partners often have intrusive memories and flashbacks and can alternate between feeling numb and becoming hyper-aroused and accusatory.

It is not too extreme to note that discovering an affair creates a crisis! It is a serious and devastating threat to your partner's security and attachment needs. Consider the extreme emotional adversity and vulnerability from isolation and separation in the events of miscarriage, death and life-threatening illnesses. This is not dissimilar.

What now? What can you do if you find yourself or your partner in an adulterous affair? Will you ever recover together, or will your marriage be irreconcilably torn apart? Like many of these extreme events, couples can recover when there is demonstrated commitment toward remorse and forgiveness. Demonstrated commitment includes an acknowledgement that a primary relationship rule has been broken. A focus on transparency, patience, reassurance and validation to repair the broken trust is required: it can take up to three years for trust to be re-established. In therapy, this usually commences with understanding who the betrayer sought to 'become' and what needs they yearned to fulfil.

We also collaborate on skills to manage flashbacks, obsessions and triggers and talk about the difference between reconciliation and forgiveness. A usual pitfall for couples in recovery is for the betrayer to downplay what has happened in their efforts to repress any shame and guilt. This causes the injured partner to repeat questions and concerns all over again, with even greater fervour. It creates a painful cycle that traps them in isolation and pain. Importantly, affair recovery recognises the needs of both partners and their longings and desires versus repeated shame for the betrayer.

The greatest possible outcome of adultery is that couples build a stronger, shiny, new and improved city of a relationship, far better than the one that was rocked in the earthquake of the affair. If couples decide to part, it is so important to unveil any resulting skewed beliefs about themselves or trusting others that can inhibit future relationships. May I highlight that it's so exciting to get fun and flirty. It is my hope, however, that this chapter has provided a warning of the consequences when you're doing it with the wrong person!

TAKEAWAY TOOLS

- Infidelity begins with small actions which grow into bigger, catastrophic disasters.
- Committing adultery is not limited to physical contact but can take many forms. If you're hiding any of your interactions with another from your partner, then there's a fair bet you're being adulterous.
- The reasons partners embark on affairs outside the relationship are many and varied, but revolve around their sense of worth and worthiness within the relationship. Open communication between the two of you is essential.
- Pornography is not necessarily a precursor to adultery but in any relationship, it needs to be sanctioned, comfortable for and welcomed by both partners.
- An affair outside a relationship is akin to the death of a loved one. It's hard to bring a body back from the dead, but breathing life into a dying relationship is possible with remorse, forgiveness and the rebuilding of trust and love.

WORDS OF WISDOM

Newly loved up couples may think a good relationship involves calm seas; an experienced couple knows it involves good seamanship.

Who Are Your Relationship Influencers?

When you're out and about with your partner, generally one half of the couple is highly unlikely to ask for directions, whilst the other is at least furiously consulting Google Maps in between repeatedly yelling at the driver to pull over and ask someone. If you're in a relationship, thinking about marriage or already married, the destination you're looking for seems pretty well cut and dried so why would you ask for the best way to get there? You're already on your way travelling toward your 'happily ever after' and despite the many forks in the road, are even less likely to ask for guidance. That is, unless you unwittingly take a wrong turn, and then another and another, while carelessly watching the scenery go by.

Despite all the trends, media and hype, people *do* still care about marriage and spend at least some time worrying about how to go about making the whole lasting committed relationship thing work. For the 'unmarrieds' who are constantly bombarded with failed marriage statistics and examples from their parents, neighbours, friends, the greengrocer and workmates who didn't last the distance, you can understand their worry. The thought of bothering with a committed relationship, even marriage, certainly seems to warrant hesitation.

As a passionate marriage counsellor who is unrelenting in her quest to inspire long-lasting relationships around the world, it has become obvious to me that our *relationship mentors* are the ones who help frame our success in achieving love and connection. The relational legacy your parents (and their parents) have left is impacting you right now and is either consciously or subconsciously and negatively or positively affecting your ability to confidently and effectively navigate your way down the Highway of Love.

Many of my clients have experienced and observed adverse relationship models and mentors in a variety of forms in their life which have had a damaging effect on their present relationships. For this reason, much of my counselling work includes motivating clients to push through any poor past generational influencers to

> There's no shame in cutting your own mistakes short by refusing to repeat someone else's! Imagine if we initially sought guidance from people who know what they're doing and are doing it well.

positively impact generations of the future, namely your children and grandchildren.

Unfortunately, we have very much evolved into an individualist society, buying into self-sufficiency and the idea that 'I know best.' I want to put it out there: there's no shame in cutting your own mistakes short by refusing to repeat someone else's! Imagine if we initially sought guidance from people who know what they're doing and are doing it well. I wonder if our roughly one in three Australian divorce rate would improve?[54]

Many of you are probably now thinking marriage counselling is a great way to go for impartial and effective advice on how to improve your relationship. I'd be lying if I didn't say much of Australian society still seems to be running under the impression that it's solely our own responsibility to sort ourselves out. There's the stigma that if anyone seeks help, they're a few cents short of a dollar. It's just plain not true. Why isn't your therapist in your well-being phone contacts along with your dentist and doctor? Luckily there's more than one way to shear a sheep and that's with the help of marriage mentors. In plainer English, the people you know or follow who are in successful, long-term, committed relationships are some of the best people you can model your relationship on.

Now, I understand there's a lot of unsolicited advice from many oldies. I think everyone knows at least one granny who has a word of wisdom or a saying for every single thing that happens in your life. Marriage mentors are more like people who realise that life isn't always a bed of roses and that relationships require a bit of watering and pruning. Even if you meet the most wonderful person in the world, your relationship is still going to require emotional attentiveness for life. Newly loved up couples may think a good relationship involves calm seas; an experienced couple knows it involves good seamanship.

What you want out of a marriage mentor is fairly simple: be around them, bask in their relationship and ask for their 'pearls of wisdom'. The idea is to seek out and surround yourself with couples whose relationships you admire. By surrounding yourselves with and watching how these couples roll, you'll start to understand their thoughts and feelings and emulate their behaviour. My parents mentored behaviours such as regular meals around the table without the TV for open discussion and the importance of carving out 'couple time' without the distraction of us!

Each mentoring relationship takes on its own style and personality. The amount of time spent with mentoring couples and the content discussed can rarely be prescribed, but there are some key benefits regardless of what format you choose:

- **They help keep you on track**

  They'll remind you how wonderful life can be when you have a loving partner by your side as well as providing a reality check on the devastating life-long consequences of bailing out too soon.

- **They won't allow you to sweat the small stuff**

  These wise elders can help put things back into perspective and remind you of what is truly important.

- **They will put a mirror in your face**

  Is your spouse always at fault? It takes two.

- **They provide a positive spin on marriage**

  These winners are defying the statistics and the world is a happier, healthier place because of them. They'll help you ward off any negative thoughts and encourage you to keep fighting for the relationship you most desire.

Marriage Mentors can help you to design your version of and keep you on the road toward your *happily ever after.*

Through the process of conducting interviews for an Australian Relationship Influencers series I wrote for the Sunshine Coast Daily, I have gleaned an incredible amount of knowledge and information from couples who have either encouraged, motivated and facilitated great relationships, set a fine example of being in one, or both! Their wisdom as exemplary relationship mentors is invaluable for anyone seeking to improve their relationship, or trying to figure out exactly what they want from one. Some of their ideas on what kept their marriage on track were incredibly simple, others more profound, but every single one of their suggestions is worth adding to your renovation blueprint. They include:

'Constantly engage in little rituals that connect' advised John Aiken, psychologist for Channel Nine's Australian *Married at First Sight* reality TV show. Successful couples make time for or prioritise each other in activities such as morning coffee, walks or a debrief together in bed at the end of the day. It's the little things that count!

'Beware of virtual infidelity' warned Clinton Power, fellow relationship therapist from Clinton Power & Associates. Many of us hold our screens as an extension of our arm. They're rarely out of sight and can lead to the temptation of secret flirting or sexting with someone outside your relationship.

'Be an open book with each other' suggested Barbara and Allan Pease, body language experts, motivational speakers and authors. They also affirmed that their relationship was always on an equal footing together financially, as business partners, as lovers and as parents.

'Shower and wear deodorant' were important and funny tips from Pastor Matt and Karryn Thiele from Immanuel Lutheran Church, Queensland. Are you retaining the best version of yourself for your partner, that self who allured them into your arms in the first place? You both deserve a fit, healthy and enticing partner to come home to.

'Prioritise the parents' was also great advice that Matt and Karryn were given and followed. 'Keep your relationship strong and your children will be secure. Never let the children divide you or think that they come first, their security comes from knowing that you two are strong. When you get home, kiss each other first before giving the children attention.' As we struggle to avoid producing the next 'entitled' Generation Z, it's not uncommon for couples I counsel to have lost each other as they gratify their children first. Inherently, they are more demanding and noisier, but succumbing to this habit too often can compromise the foundation of the family: the love between the parents.

'Relish and learn from the example set by role models': Marriage celebrant Jacqui Clarke and her husband Graham both had incredible parent influencers. It is such a gift when we've had the benefit of watching fine relationship and life mentors. My fervour for counselling is fuelled by the positive ripple effect couples instil in their children. It is my greatest desire for couples to be comfortable to disagree and show future generations how to navigate these challenges with kindness, patience and respect.

'Establish the ritual of quality dinner time as a family': Joanne Desmond, Channel Seven news presenter and husband John Smeaton, owner of the Hampton Chair Co have established dinner time habits for their family that ensure research-proven benefits for their children.[55] These include healthier eating habits, improved speech and improved mental well-being. Joanne and John state that this is their favourite part of the day as it allows them to share their thoughts and opinions and have a good laugh with their four boys, facilitating an open and honest relationship with them. The boys know that nothing is off-limits and that they can talk to them about anything without judgement.

'Compatible work ethic': This is a theme that shone through from Roz and Michael White, IGA Proprietors. Together they've honoured friendship whilst having children and maintaining a tenacious, hardworking ethic in a highly competitive industry that has produced a three-store-strong IGA empire.

'Choose your life partner wisely' recommends Ted O'Brien, Australian Federal Member for Fairfax and wife Sophia, a lecturer in law at the Sunshine Coast University. Ted is grateful that he got it so right, emphasising this as the single biggest and most influential decision you make as it will change the course of the rest of your life! I loved the way Sophia uses technology to their advantage to ensure Ted receives cute updates from their daughter and son whilst he's away in Parliament. Another 'gem' from Ted's mum (one of his marriage mentors), was this: 'Think of marriage as a shiny, golden ball. Every harsh word or thoughtless gesture creates a dent or a scratch that may be hard to erase.'

'Make the most of limited time': This is the beautiful message from my final over-achieving influencers, Doctor Sophie Poulter, a specialist in endocrinology and obstetric medicine and husband Doctor Rohan Poulter, Clinical Director of Cardiology at the Sunshine Coast University Hospital in Queensland, Australia. Their incredibly demanding and competing work schedules could easily override their relationship and family time with their three young boys but despite this, they hold hands in public, ensure regular date nights and even steal a few moments to have lunch together as well. The theme of little moments meaning so much could be heard continually throughout their interview.

Interestingly, I asked every interviewee about technology trends and the impact that phones, tablets, computers and television had had on how they maintained their relationships. Again, the message was repeated over and over that whilst the use of technology in our daily lives does have advantages, screens also have the potential to kill relationships.

> If you haven't had great relationship mentors in your childhood, now is the time to seek them out either within your family, social circle or online: find some now, read about them and learn to be one! It is never too late to begin.

If you haven't had great relationship mentors in your childhood, now is the time to seek them out either within your family, social circle or online: find some now, read about them and learn to be one! It is never too late to begin.

Therapy on Trend

As someone who desires a better relationship with your partner, you have taken commendable steps in gaining real insight into why your relationship may be lacking the love and intimacy you had back at the start and how you might go about changing the aspects of your relationship which are not working well just by reading this book. Now, imagine the power of unleashing the torrent of thoughts and emotions whirring around in your mind without fear of judgement.

What if you could metaphorically punch those words out in the air with an unbiased professional to gain clarity for healthy decision making and flourishing relationships? As someone in a marriage (with a husband I don't always agree with) who works with a wide variety of couples from all walks of life, I am always stunned when I hear of partners who are dead set against seeking out help to resolve, repair or even nurture their relationships which are so often at breaking point. If your leg was broken, you wouldn't ignore it, stick a Band-Aid over it or yell at it to get better. You would find the appropriate professional to help you and quick-smart! Why then, wouldn't you seek out similar professional help to heal another necessary and fulfilling part of your life?

Some people buy into the stigma about counselling. In Australia, therapy is often regarded as something for 'crazy' people, more commonly known in Aussie slang as 'nut-bags'. Nothing could be further from the truth. Therapy has the power to transform lives, save relationships and treat mental illness. Current research has shown that without a doubt, what therapists do in psychotherapy is incredibly effective on a neurobiological level.[56] Research suggests that around 30% of Americans have been to therapy at least once and 80% of those found it effective.[57] Why not follow these savvy people who actively seek assistance

> The exciting part of psychotherapy is gaining an external perspective to help choose those parts of your family culture you wish to flourish for future generations and those you don't.

to improve areas of their life. This help may come in the form of support, information, guidance, self-awareness and/or the space to learn and practice new tools.

If you or a 'friend' are on the fence about therapy, it's time to make up your mind and consider seeking help to achieve the life of your dreams. Here are some reasons therapy is on-trend according to your passionate-about-happy-relationships marriage counsellor, me!:

It's the preferred choice of the privileged

If you envision a person in therapy, you may well picture a wild, crazy person! In some cultures, however, therapy is synonymous with celebrity and money. These clever and prosperous people routinely seek out therapy because they know it helps propel them to the life they want. If you admire those you consider successful and famous, you'd be well-served to follow their lead.

It helps you achieve your dreams

Everyone feels stuck from time to time. There's no magic pill to help achieve your dreams, and no one else can meet your goals for you! You are the expert in your life. A counsellor, though, can help sort out what's holding you back and empower you to stop procrastinating and to begin living the life you want.

You focus on holistic health

Anxiety, depression and stress are all correlated with obesity and poor health, not to mention dying younger! Talking therapies help to affect neural activation through chemical balance, neural firing, neural structure and neural networks. In a safe and trusted environment, your stress response is down-regulated to encourage new habits that allow you to relate in new improved and resilient ways, facilitating greater control for a happier life.

Psychotherapy means better relationships

No relationship is perfect and we all have room for improvement. You and your partner—not your parents, your bank account, or your job—control the direction of your relationship. Counselling helps heal insecure attachment styles, fostering healthy relationships. A therapist can help sort through your role to arrive at a happier, more loving relationship, not to mention a better sex life.

Break family cycles

Like it or not, our childhood environment shapes so much of who we are. The exciting part of psychotherapy is gaining an external perspective to help choose those parts of your family culture you wish to flourish for future generations and those you don't. Furthermore, you can learn to provide healthy mentoring and make conscious choices about the best possible care for your children.

Counselling clients ARE normal

Just as you go to the doctor or dentist for your annual check-up even when you feel fine, a regular session with a therapist can serve as a check-in for your emotional health and you may just gain a fresh new perspective.

Choose your therapist wisely. Check their qualifications, seek out recommendations and ensure they are a member of a relevant association.

The only way to end the stigma of therapy is to be willing to try it yourself. If you need help sorting out your goals, achieving dynamic and flourishing relationships, or just getting better control of your emotions, therapy can help. Many are worried that if their partner is confronted by therapy, they won't benefit from going alone. This is not the case: you can always be the champion of change. Enjoy the therapeutic, sacred and safe space to talk alone. In time there's every chance your other half will be right there beside you.

If you're living in a remote area or for whatever reason can't get to a face-to-face session, online therapy is readily available these days, as are my online courses and resources. Therapy changes lives for the better every day and it can change yours too. It is never too late to begin journeying on the path to renewed happiness!

TAKEAWAY TOOLS

Your relationship renovation maintenance is not simply a onetime affair. Working through the tough times is a given. It's rather like staying abreast of peeling paint from the blistering sun and expecting a few fallen trees on your roof from the turbulent storms. There will always be extreme seasons, challenges and stressors in your long life together, but keeping your power tools charged, approaching issues with resilience whilst supporting each other and regularly reminding yourselves of your commitment to your relationship is an essential blueprint to maintaining joy and happiness with your partner.

- Break any negative legacies you and your partner have accrued through your lives, and be the best possible example of a loving, committed and trusting relationship for your children. Your positive legacy will shine on through them.
- Seek out and surround yourselves with your own positive marriage mentors. These people help and remind you to strive to be the best couple you can be.
- You are not alone and your problems are not insurmountable. Seek out a counsellor for relationship help.

POST RELATIONSHIP RENOVATION

Collaborating on goals and resolutions can also work towards either partner's boundaries within your relationship being respected and upheld.

Your Skyscraper Is Not Your Limit

Everyone knows change takes effort. After all, if change was easy, we'd all be mighty perfect. Now that you've gone through the extensive process of renovating your relationship, it's time to set future goals. Even if it simply means improving ourselves further, this typically involves stepping *way* outside our comfort zones. Heck, you've renovated your relationship, so you've already pushed past multiple challenges despite the temptation to whack a heavy rug over the floor boards creaking in your old dilapidated ways instead. Our brains certainly enjoy helping us stay in the 'comfort of our discomfort'. It's familiar and way too easy. One of the greatest benefits of finding a partner for life and making a commitment to them is that you have someone who is always going to work with you to achieve your goals, both individually and as a couple.

Maybe you've done the hard work and breathed life back into

your relationship. The fresh breeze is billowing through your freshly painted love nest. Don't stop there though, as it's awesome when couples collaborate on their goals and dreams in the right way and achieve even more as a team. Remember, we are not here to complete the other person nor are we in competition with each other. Couples are not just compatible: you are complementary. It's time to take advantage of the inherent strengths each of you brings to your relationship to become a united force, accomplishing those goals and dreams you'd otherwise struggle to achieve on your own. You need each other!

Achieving goals is a pretty great thing. It helps grow you as a person and instils a sense of purpose. If you set some mutual goals with your partner you can grow a deeper connection through shared effort. There are two major benefits of teaming up with your partner and approaching your dreams and desires together:

- It's been proven that people who wrote out their goals with an action plan and sent it to a supportive friend, reported a significantly higher level of success than those who just wrote or thought about their goals.[58] You already have a supportive someone: they're sitting right there next to you!

- In a relationship, you also get a chance to work out your healthy boundaries around independence and interdependence. You're still two individual human beings: embrace your differences and support each other in your respective pursuits.

Goals shouldn't just be focussed around your dream job or next holiday destination either. Collaborating on goals and resolutions can also work towards either partner's boundaries within your relationship being respected and upheld. For example, you might discuss your sex life and your arguments with your mates: you're all friends, you share stories, you know the deal. Understandably, though, your partner might really not want Davo or Christine to know about what you get up to in the bedroom.

Setting a goal of 'I won't discuss our private life with my next-door neighbour unless it's agreed first', is a really easy way to respect your partner's boundaries. Is there are a limit to the way you'll allow yourself to be spoken to, before you feel you're being disrespected? That's a boundary, too. Do you need to talk about working toward new approaches to social media and screen usage again? They're perfectly healthy boundaries that relationships need.

It's important to openly discuss what you're both trying to achieve, individually and together. Celebrate your different goals! There's no point in tip-toeing around topics when you're discussing your hopes, dreams and aspirations, but honesty is paramount. If you agree to

> It takes about 30 repetitions to move out of the comfort of your discomfort towards a new positive habit so expect over a month for these new behaviours to be wired.

something but you actually feel it goes against your best interests or values, it's going to come crashing down in flames later. Speaking of which, don't shoot down ideas in the planning stage without hearing them out first. No rolling of the eyes, huffing or grunting is allowed during your brainstorming and bucket list creation time together.

Both partners need to have a chance to say their piece and explain their desires. If something doesn't mutually work for both of you, talk it through or maybe place it a little lower on the agenda for now. Take advantage of my handy little chart at www.relationshiprejuvenator.com/goalsetting.

Once you've decided on your goals both together and individually, acknowledge that your brain will often default to remembering even one bad experience around lack of goal achievement over the multitude of times when you've succeeded! It takes about 30 repetitions to move out of the comfort of your discomfort to-

> Mutual encouragement, support and celebration is key to both of you reaching targets and growing stronger together.

wards a new positive habit so expect over a month for these new behaviours to be wired. Neurons that fire together wire together so ensure repetition and consistency:

Make goals specific, actionable and in full view

Make them targeted to something realistic and explicit rather than shooting for the stars. Your noggin can't conceptualise vague, up-in-the-airy fairy ideas!

Handwrite them

This externalises your ideas and uses thousands of movements which create heavier mental lifting for new neural pathways in your brain. It's been said that students are over 40% more likely to learn more this way.[59]

State them in the positive

Don't use negative wording such as, 'I won't engage in X anymore.' Start your sentences with 'I will be X by Y.' For example, most resolutions about health and weight loss happen after the festive season, but deciding 'I will eat healthier food' isn't exactly an actionable goal. You have to work towards it in increments and allow your brain to visualise it. This is why you need specific strategies that will step you toward your ultimate goal. Want to be healthier? Make it your goal to eat X less fast food meals a week. Make it a goal to go to the gym X times a week. This way, you have actioned toward your goal of being healthier in an accountable way.

Visualise it on your big screen

See yourself parading around with more energy and zest wearing stripes, white or your new jumpsuit or whatever does it for you!

Neon lights

If you both keep your goals highlighted around your pad where the other will notice, it will help spur you to action. Pasting up your goals on the back of the toilet door and above the kitchen sink allows your brain to view constructive images of your outcomes with clarity. When it's in your face, watch your motivation fire up! Have I mentioned repetition and consistency?

There's one other important thing couples need to do: support each other and celebrate your achievements! There's nothing worse than striving for something that's been a great personal challenge only for your partner to be completely apathetic about your progress. Mutual encouragement, support and celebration is key to both of you reaching targets and growing stronger together.

Goals and resolutions don't have to be huge. They don't have to be about becoming famous illusionists or crypto currency experts by next month. Whilst some of those are worthy, they can be about the little things in life that we might need to work on to make ourselves stay true to our values or just better partners. It's such a great time to address, reinforce or simply discuss setting some of these healthy boundaries. They'll help bolster your relationship and leave you all the stronger for it.

Finally, recognise the components of a habit: the cue, the action and the reward. Keep your ideals simple and straight forward and get good quality sleep for better brain function, wellness and resilience, then go for it tenaciously as a united force! Your skyscraper is not your limit.

Reset and Start Afresh?

Strictly speaking, counsellors don't have an opinion. However, for those individuals and couples who are diligently using the relevant Toolbox Tools throughout this book, you may be feeling like you need confirmation that you are at least investing correctly in the right direction. I have an idea to help you step your renovation up to the next level. It's a suggestion for those already married, one that's not necessarily expensive to do and can be as big or little, as public or private as you like. It brings you back to why you signed up for this whole thing in the first place. It's not a new concept and admittedly, it is one I had previously considered a little cheesy and pointless and more of an excuse to 'look at me'.

Toolbox Topic Nine: Post Relationship Renovation

That was until I journeyed with a couple in therapy who'd been confronted by major relationship trauma. They sought to start the new year fresh and connected, quite literally drawing a line in the pristine sand of an idyllic beach to mark the building of a brand-new shiny castle of a relationship, one standing on a solid foundation of the greater understanding and growth they'd achieved through significant adversity the year prior. And they invited me along.

This couple gave me the honour of officiating the renewal of their vows on a glorious New Year's Day morning accompanied by one friend, a camera, their beautiful children and some personal touches on their local beach. Not only was I thrilled to revel in the joy of contributing to this couple's awe-inspiring journey, but I was amazed at their tenacity and strength to intentionally forgive and turn toward each other through this beautiful ritual. As you could imagine, it was emotional. I loved them, I loved the ritual, I loved my role in it and I loved this poignant start to the year!

Renewing your vows with your partner is an incredibly powerful custom, one that should be given just as much gravity if not more than the first time you did it. This is not one of the 'little things' you do regularly to nurture your relationship, but one of those 'big' moments, another high point in your life together which celebrates you as a couple:

- It can be a powerful re-anchoring of each promise you gave to each other. Did you have any idea what you entered into all starry-eyed way back when?
- Many couples can spend hundreds of hours planning their wedding, not so many hours writing their vows and like me, barely remember them. (Did I really say obey?)

- How many of us revisit our vows? A vow renewal is a wonderful reason to dig them out and spend a bit more time crafting or integrating the original script with a new version, one which might be based on your experiences now that you've been through a bit of sickness and health. You might be richer or poorer and likely delighted, disappointed and sometimes disillusioned by them.

> You are encouraged to assess and review your contribution to the marriage. Have you created an enviable, quality-laden marriage that any children could be mentored from and that will positively impact generations to come?

- Those vows are then more likely to be at the forefront of your text messages, birthday cards and daily interactions. The words are re-ignited with on-going life.
- Rather than see the marriage commitment and its related promises as a given, you are reminded to recognise how your union will shift and change and you can in turn honour the right for it to do so.
- As an annual ritual, it helps you intentionally make that decision to be the best spouse you can be even on those days you might slightly dislike them.
- You are encouraged to assess and review your contribution to the marriage. Have you created an enviable, quality-laden marriage that any children could be mentored from and that will positively impact generations to come?
- There are some wild and wonderful locations to use as a

gob-smacking backdrop to your special occasion or simply use the privacy of the current love-pad you've built together.

- Now go celebrate!

If this is not your first marriage, then there is even more reason to invest your time in this process for a marked differential. Ask a special friend or family member to officiate. Go with a professional celebrant for all the on-trend professional bells and whistles. I've officiated once now so surely that makes me an expert? Happy to be at your service. I'll bring tissues this time...

TAKEAWAY TOOLS

Whilst you may have breathed life back into your relationship, it's worthwhile to align yourselves with a plan.

- Stand together in support of your independent and interdependent goals. You will achieve more, feel greater satisfaction and flourish together.
- Consider renewing your marriage or commitment vows as a way of grounding and celebrating the love, trust and companionship you have with each other.

TIME FOR ACTION ON THOSE TWO WORDS

I desire that you work hard to overcome your past pitfalls: otherwise you risk finding another version of your behaviours and a similar dynamic in your next romance.

There you have it! You now have all the power tools you'll need for a successful, fulfilling relationship—time to put it all into practice. As with all strategies employed in the counselling room, make your key aha moments in this book visual so it is not a case of 'set on your shelf, kindle or audiobook and forget'. I encourage you to continually refer back to the key tools in the book and take advantage of the resources at www.relationshiprejuvenator.com.

Remember what it was that attracted you to each other in the first place? You may have experienced the 'I-can't-breathes' from the rush of attraction and love in the early days, but now you *can* breathe (likely with a heavy sigh sometimes). Time, children, stress, challenges and laziness will all wear down and even shake your 'Love Shack'. Through taking ownership of how you are *both* dealing with being on the tools, you should be able to work through those rough storms fully rigged with all the equipment and patience required to maintain or rebuild. If you have children, will you be able to convey at their future milestone celebrations that you fought tooth and nail for *your* admirable relationship which provided a stable foundation to help launch their success?

The relationship legacy left by your parents and your past does not define you, but it will be present in both your conscious and subconscious mind. It will therefore affect your actions today, regardless of whether you rail against that legacy, eventually succumb to and repeat it, or choose to take on board the positive aspects to make your marriage or committed relationship the best it can be. Either way, working out what *is* working for you both and aspiring to present the best possible example of a loving, caring and supportive relationship to your children, should be the ultimate goal. As a wonderful side effect, you'll join the crowd of other thriving couples with a head start on longevity, good health and contentment consistent with all those happiness studies.

The scientific facts are that we all need love: partnering up with your 'forever after' person is a traditional method of ensuring love is a part of every single day of your life, not to mention providing companionship, someone who'll help you pull your kids into line and support you through life's inevitable ups and downs. When we first find our other half, the excitement is overwhelming but as the years roll by, children may come along and the general melee of life throws its punches at you, and that excitement can be replaced with apathy and even aversion. It is not acceptable to simply move on from your marriage at this stage! You need to invest in your relationship, and sometimes that means taking a good hard look at yourself. If you've given this your all, you will at least have peace moving forward whether it is together or apart.

Toolbox Topic Ten: Time for Action on Those Two Words

Your 'Blame Game' needs to be re-engineered so feedback is delivered and received in a non-blaming way. Any attempt at revitalising a marriage must begin with introspection and most often a painfully truthful answer to the question, *Am I giving the best version of myself to my partner and this relationship?* Usually you are not, for a variety of reasons including stress, an unwillingness to forgive, fixed methods of communication styles, the impact of your relationship observations in the past (including the legacy of your parents) and other fall-out from traumatic events, influences or habits. It's a long list! Commitment to your marriage and your relationship, however, requires you to do something about it in order to make your partnership a joyful place once more. The way we communicate (or don't communicate!) is all too often the main culprit in a marriage shifting from one of peaches and cream to one of sour lemons.

Be curious that our brains communicate via our unique, mosaic blend of masculine and feminine brain features. Have tolerance for different kinds of communication—from 'Just give me the bare facts' to 'Here are the facts + copious amounts of detail'. We are gloriously different: embrace it! For many couples, unfortunately authentic conversation has been replaced with white noise about schedules, bills, children, monosyllabic grunts or worse, screens. For some, withholding communication has become a way of building those walls against the perceived threat of becoming hurt and the only way of breaking those walls down is with courageous vulnerability and conversation. Those things we can't live without—screens—are also becoming a major relationship-communication buster. Stop phubbing your partner, put your phone down and talk to each other.

When relationships are at breaking point, however, more is needed than simply 'talking it through'. Infidelity of the emotional, physical or financial kind will bring a relationship to rock bottom. This is a humbling place where remorse and forgiveness are the only actions that might give a little light to a hopeful recovery. Your sole option is to tread together through the painful glass and debris toward repair. When true remorse and eventual forgiveness exist, then with mutual hard work you *will* be able to build a more magnificent, transformed and completely renovated structure of a relationship than was ever experienced before.

Years and years of apathy, endless criticisms and ignoring 'bids' for attentiveness will eventually destroy your marriage and zest for life. When respect, kindness and appreciation has gone out the window, your renovation rescue is perilously built on rubble! For people in this situation, consulting an impartial professional who is educated and experienced in guiding you out of that black hole is the most effective way of bringing joy, fun and happiness back into your marriage and into your life. I ask you to ensure you have peace in knowing that you are giving your current relationship your absolute all. I desire that you work hard to overcome your past pitfalls: otherwise you risk finding another version of your behaviours and a similar dynamic in your next romance. They may not be evident at the start but could well manifest later so it is worth turning your attention to losing any existing unhelpful ways right now!

And for those couples with just a few pain points, I'm pleased to say that maintaining your relationship residence doesn't ever end! You will need to restore it regularly with gratitude, actual time together, inspiring role models and a focus on being the best you; how wonderful is that!? This should not be viewed as a never-ending painful grind of tolerating each other but instead a process of lovingly and attentively tending to the relationship garden surrounding your carefully maintained palace of love.

We all thrive on that amazing feeling of love and connection. Marriage is a wonderful tradition which combines that love along with commitment and lifelong support and where happiness, fun and companionship can live forever with the person who, at some time, rocked your foundations. Giving up on that is unthinkable so why not create a rock-solid foundation for a lifetime of passion and respect and nurture a thriving and dynamic relationship that impacts generations.

Hold onto these power tools for love, keep them charged and TRI Bonding.

For a full suite of supporting resources, your relationship rejuvenation continues here: www.relationshiprejvuenator.com.

Renovate Your Relationship

⌂ ENDNOTES

¹ Mark Batterson, Draw the Circle: The 40 Day Prayer Challenge, Zondervan Dec. 2012.

² Compassionate Communities UK (n.d.) retrieved from <https://www.compassionate-communitiesuk.co.uk/projects>

³ John B. Arden. *Mind-Brain-Gene: Toward Psychotherapy Integration*. WW Norton & Co, 2019.

⁴ Douglas Institute *Childhood trauma has life-long effect on genes and the brain.* Retrieved from <https://www.mcgill.ca/newsroom/channels/news/childhood-trauma-has-life-long-effect-genes-and-brain-104667> February 22, 2009.

⁵ M Filkowski, R Cochran, B Hass, *Altruistic Behaviour: Mapping Responses in the Brain,* Neurosci Neuroecon. 2016; 5: pp65—75.

⁶ William T. Harbaugh, Ulrich Mayr and Dan Burghart. *Neural Responses to Taxation and Voluntary Giving Reveal Motives for Charitable Donations.* Science, June 15, 2007.

⁷ Nicholas H Wolfinger, *Does Having Children Make People Happier in the Long Run?* Institute of Family Studies, 2018. Retrieved from <https://ifstudies.org/blog/does-having-children-make-people-happier-in-the-long-run>

⁸ Nicholas H Wolfinger, *Does Having Children Make People Happier in the Long Run?* Institute of Family Studies, 2018. Retrieved from <https://ifstudies.org/blog/does-having-children-make-people-happier-in-the-long-run>

[9] Wendy D Manning. *Cohabitation and Child Wellbeing.* Future Child. 2015 Fall; 25(2): 51–66. Retrieved from https://www.ncbi.nlm.nih.gov/pmc/articles/PMC4768758/

[10] Brown Susan L, Rinelli Lauren N. *Family Structure, Family Processes, and Adolescent Smoking and Drinking.* Journal of Research on Adolescence. 2010;20:pp259–273.

[11] Andrew K.Shenton, *Viewing information needs through a Johari Window,* Retrieved from <https://www.emerald.com/insight/content/doi/10.1108/00907320710774337/full/html> August 2007

[12] Jen Wilkin, *Women of the World.* Crossway, Wheaton, Illinois, 2014, p31.

[13] Dr Caroline Leaf, *Think and Eat Yourself Smart.* Baker Books, 2016.

[14] Dr Caroline Leaf, *Think and Eat Yourself Smart.* Baker Books, 2016, p84

[15] 8 Simple Steps to Build Up Your Stress Resilience. Retrieved from <https://drleaf.com/blogs/news/8-simple-steps-to-build-up-your-stress-resilience> June 26, 2019

[16] Dr Caroline Leaf. *Switch on Your Brain: The Key to Peak Happiness, Thinking and Health.* Baker Books, 2015.

[17] Dr Caroline Leaf, *Why You Should Embrace the Forgiveness Mindset* (n.d.). Retrieved from <https://thriveglobal.com/stories/why-you-should-embrace-the-forgiveness-mindset/>

[18] S Freedman, T Zarifkar, *The Psychology of Interpersonal Forgiveness and Guidelines for Forgiveness Therapy: What Therapists Need to Know to Help Their Clients Forgive.* Spirituality in Clinical Practice, Vol 3, No 1, pp45—48. (n.d.).

[19] Everett L. Worthington Jr, *The New Science of Forgiveness.* (n.d.) Retrieved from <https://greatergood.berkeley.edu/article/item/the_new_science_of_forgiveness>

[20] Gary Chapman, *The Five Love Languages: How to Express Heartfelt Commitment to Your Mate.* Northfield Publishing, 1992.

Endnotes

[21] Laurie Watson. *Wanting Sex Again: How to Rediscover Your Desire and Heal a Sexless Marriage.* Berkley Books, 2012.

[22] Dr Sarah McKay, The Women's Brain Book, Hachette Australia, Sydney 2018, p8.

[23] Dr Sarah McKay, The Women's Brain Book, Hachette Australia, Sydney 2018. Retrieved from <https://www.abc.net.au/radionational/programs/allinthemind/womens-brains/9711718>

[24] Dr Sarah McKay, *The Women's Brain, The Neuroscience of Health, Hormones and Happiness.* Hachette Australia, 2018. p12.

[25] Helen Rowland on Quotes.net (n.d.) retrieved from <https://www.quotes.net/quote/17116>

[26] Dr Caroline Leaf, *Who Switched off Your Brain? Solving the Mystery of He Said, She Said.* Thomas Nelson Incorporated, 2006, p24.

[27] Dr Caroline Leaf, *Who Switched off Your Brain? Solving the Mystery of He Said, She Said.* Thomas Nelson Incorporated, 2006. p64.

[28] Dr Caroline Leaf, *Who Switched off Your Brain? Solving the Mystery of He Said, She Said.* Thomas Nelson Incorporated, 2006. p52.

[29] The Gottman Institute: *Want to Improve Your Relationship?* (n.d.) retrieved from <https://checkup.gottman.com/>

[30] The Gottman Institute. *Turn Towards Instead of Away* retrieved from <https://www.gottman.com/blog/turn-toward-instead-of-away/> 2015.

[31] Liz Mineo *Good Genes Are Nice, But Joy Is Better.* The Harvard Gazette, April 2017. Retrieved from https://news.harvard.edu/gazette/story/2017/04/over-nearly-80-years-harvard-study-has-been-showing-how-to-live-a-healthy-and-happy-life/

[32] Stan Tatkin, *Our Automatic Brain: Everything New Will Soon Be Old.* Retrieved from <https://stantatkinblog.wordpress.com/2015/04/02/our-automatic-brain-everything-new-will-soon-be-old/>

[33] Prepare Enrich: Building Strong Relationships (n.d.) Available from <https://www.prepare-enrich.com.au/>

[34] The Gottman Institute *Relationship Check-up.* (n.d.) Retrieved from <https://checkup.gottman.com/>

[35] Gary Chapman, *The Five Love Languages: How to Express Heartfelt Commitment to Your Mate.* Northfield Publishing, 1992.

[36] Matthew Thiele, *Intrinsic Affirmation And Marriage Satisfaction for Australian Institute Of Family Counselling,* April 2020, p4.

[37] Matthew Thiele, *Intrinsic Affirmation And Marriage Satisfaction for Australian Institute Of Family Counselling,* April 2020, p10.

[38] Relationships Australia February 2015 *The Internet and Relationships.* Retrieved from <https://www.relationships.org.au/what-we-do/research/online-survey/february-2015-the-internet-and-relationships>

[39] Ruhr-Universität Bochum (RUB) led by Dr. Phillip Ozimek *Behaviour & Information Technology.* Neuroscience News, 12 July 2019. Retrieved from < https://neurosciencenews.com/facebook-use-depression-14523/>

[40] Relationships Australia February 2015 *The Internet and Relationships.* retrieved from <https://www.relationships.org.au/what-we-do/research/online-survey/february-2015-the-internet-and-relationships>

[41] Nicholas H Wolfinger, *Does Having Children Make People Happier in the Long Run?* Institute of Family Studies, 2018. Retrieved from <https://ifstudies.org/blog/does-having-children-make-people-happier-in-the-long-run>

[42] Yoo Rha Hong and Jae Sun Park, *Impact of attachment, temperament and parenting on human development.* Korean Journal of Paediatrics, 2012. 55 (12): pp449—454.

Endnotes

[43] Dr Sarah McKay, *The Women's Brain, The Neuroscience of Health, Hormones and Happiness.* Hachette Australia, 2018, p194.

[44] Dr Dan Siegel, Interview: *Understanding the Teenage Brain.* Australian Counselling. (n.d.) Retrieved from <https://www.australiacounselling.com.au/understanding-teenage-brain-dr-dan-siegel/>

[45] Dr Caroline Leaf, *Milkshake multitasking reduces intelligence.* (n.d.) Retrieved from <https://www.facebook.com/drleaf/videos/10153591011996078/>

[46] Australian Government, Australian Institute of Family Studies. *Divorce Rates in Australia.* (n.d.) Retrieved from <https://aifs.gov.au/facts-and-figures/divorce-rates-australia>

[47] Prepare Enrich: Building Strong Relationships (n.d.) Retrieved from <https://www.prepare-enrich.com.au/>

[48] Dr Shirley Glass, *Not Just Friends: Rebuilding Trust and Recovering Sanity After Infidelity.* Atria Books, 2004.

[49] Relationship Institute Australasia. Counselling and Professional Training Workshop.(n.d.) *Let's Talk Infidelity and Trauma.*

[50] *Pornhub 2019 A Year in Review.* Retrieved from <https://www.pornhub.com/insights/2019-year-in-review>

[51] Dr Bryant Paul PhD and Dr Jae Woong Shim, *Gender, Sexual Affect, and Motivations for Internet Pornography Use.* International Journal of Sexual Health, 2008 20:3, pp187—199.

[52] Dr Clare Rosoman, *Emotionally Focussed Couples Therapy and Pornography: Threat or Tool?* Training workshop, 2017.

[53] Dr Debby Herbenick, *Sex Made Easy: Your Awkward Questions Answered For Better, Smarter, Amazing Sex.* Running Press, 2012.

[54] Australian Bureau of Statistics, 2018. *Marriages and Divorces, Australia 2018.* Retrieved from <https://www.abs.gov.au/ausstats/abs@.nsf/mf/3310.0>

[55] The Australian Parenting Website. *Family Rituals: What Are They?* Raising Children.(n.d.) Accessed from <https://raisingchildren.net.au/grown-ups/family-life/routines-rituals-relationships/family-rituals>

[56] Pieter Rossouw, *The Interconnectedness of Us: Neuroscience Mirror Neurons and Talking Therapies.* Keynote speech. September 2013. Retrieved from <https://www.researchgate.net/publication/268448051_The_Interconnectedness_of_us_-_Neuroscience_mirror_neurons_and_talking_therapies_Keynote>

[57] *Survey says: More Americans are seeking mental health treatment.* American Psychological Association. July/August 2004, Vol 35, No 7. p17.

[58] Dr. Gail Matthews, *Study focuses on strategies for achieving goals, resolutions.* Dominican University of California (n.d.) Retrieved from <https://scholar.dominican.edu/cgi/viewcontent.cgi?article=1265&context=news-releases>

[59] Pam A. Mueller and Daniel M Oppenheimer, *The Pen is Mightier Than the Keyboard: Advantages of Longhand Over Laptop Note Taking.* Psychological Science. Sage Publishing, Vol 25(4) pp1159—1168, 2014.

ABOUT THE AUTHOR

Joanne Wilson is a professional counsellor and psycho-therapist, author, speaker and a renowned pioneer in her field. The founder of The Confidante Counselling, Relationship Rejuvenator online courses and a specialist in relationships and pre-marriage therapy, Joanne was the first Australian counsellor to create her own relationship app. You can find all her incredible resources at: www.relationshiprejuvenator.com.

Her innovative TRI Bonding model is revolutionising the way couples view their relationships and she is passionate about creating generational change by encouraging couples to truly give their marriages the attention they deserve.

Joanne is the relationships feature columnist for the Sunshine Coast Daily, a co-host on radio station Salt106.5, and a contributor for various local and national newspapers including the Melbourne Sun Herald and countless radio stations. Her beautiful relationships coffee table book *Pearls of Wisdom from the Thriving Thirties*, developed in collaboration with the Immanuel Lutheran Church community and others, highlights the wisdom and experience of our older generation in maintaining healthy relationships.

With broad life exposure including overseas training and diverse work experiences across Australia, she has refined the skill of being a non-judgemental and highly regarded practitioner. With caring, compassion and patience she has been acknowledged as a respected counsellor with a balanced career alongside family and community contributions.

Motivated by a passion for holistic wellbeing, she continues to develop resources, seminars and the online Relationship Rejuvenator website and courses that enable people of all ages to develop and maintain positive, lasting relationships.

Joanne developed her nurturing, patient-driven approach through extensive community services work, including with the homeless at Wayside Chapel in Kings Cross, Sydney and troubled young women at Mercy Ministries and Lily House on the Sunshine Coast.

www.ingramcontent.com/pod-product-compliance
Lightning Source LLC
Chambersburg PA
CBHW021859020426
42334CB00013B/399